ISBN 978-1-332-41048-4
PIBN 10423602

1 MONTH OF
FREE
READING

at
www.ForgottenBooks.com

By purchasing this book you are eligible for one month membership to ForgottenBooks.com, giving you unlimited access to our entire collection of over 1,000,000 titles via our web site and mobile apps.

To claim your free month visit:

www.forgottenbooks.com/free423602

TO THE

GENERAL FEDERATION OF WOMEN'S CLUBS

IN AMERICA

THIS BOOK IS AFFECTIONATELY DEDICATED

BY

THE WOMAN'S PRESS CLUB

OF

NEW YORK CITY

Foreword

ON January 6, 1902, a Memorial Meeting was called by Sorosis jointly with the Woman's Press Club of New York City, and a month later the Press Club formally authorized the preparation of a Memorial Book to its Founder and continuous President to the day of her death, Jane Cunningham Croly.

In addition to a biographical sketch to be prepared by her brother, the Rev. John Cunningham, this book, so it was planned, should contain such letters, or excerpts from letters, as would illustrate her lovable personality and her life philosophy.

A Committee of Publication was appointed, consisting of Mrs. Caroline M. Morse, Chairman, Mrs. Mary Coffin Johnson, Mrs. Haryot Holt Dey, Mrs. Miriam Mason Greeley, Miss Anna Warren Story and Mrs. Margaret W. Ravenhill. These began their work by sending a printed slip to club members and to Mrs. Croly's known intimates, asking for her letters. But the response came almost without variation: " My letters from Mrs. Croly are of too personal a nature for publication." A few, however, were freely offered, and these it was decided should be used, depending for the bulk of the Memorial upon copious extracts from Mrs. Croly's "History of the Woman's Club Movement in America," from her editorial work on *The Cycle*, and from her miscellaneous writings. To this characteristic material her long cherished friends, Mr. and Mrs. Thaddeus B. Wakeman, added an account of the "Positivist Episode," that objective point in her career, with which her husband was closely identified.

With these are: Mrs. Croly's Club Life, a sketch by Mrs. Haryot Holt Dey; the Sorosis-Press Club Memorial Meeting; the Resolutions of the Woman's Press Club of New York City, the General Federation of Clubs, and the Society of American Women in London; tributes from London clubwomen; Essays and Addresses; Letters and Stray Leaves and Notes, written by Mrs. Croly; tributes from many of her friends, and my own recollections.

CAROLINE M. MORSE,
                                    Chairman.

Contents

Contents

Illustrations

Jenny June

The South Wind blows across the harrowed fields,
  And lo! the young grain springs to happy birth;
His warm breath lingers where the granite shields
  Intruding flowers, and the responsive Earth
Impartially her varied harvest yields.
  Through long ensuing months with tender mirth
  The South Wind laughs, rejoicing in the worth
Of the impellent energies he wields.

  Within our minds the memory of a Name
Will move, and fires of inspiration that burned low
  Among dead embers break in quickening flame;
Flowers of the soul, grain of the heart shall grow,
And burgeoned promises shall bravely blow
  Beneath the sunny influence of Her fame.

                              ETHEL MORSE

xi

A Brother's Memories

A Brother's Memories

By John Cunningham, D.D.

THE most interesting and potent fact within the range of human knowledge is personality, and in the person of Jane Cunningham Croly (Jenny June) a potency was apparent which has affected the social life of more women, perhaps, than any other single controlling factor of the same period.

Jane Cunningham was born in Market Harborough, Leicestershire, England, December 19, 1829. She was the fourth child of Joseph H. and Jane Cunningham, and though small in stature and delicate in organism, was full of vivacity, and abounding in natural intelligence. Her rich brown hair, blue eyes and clear complexion proclaimed her of Anglo-Saxon origin. She was the idol of her parents and the admiration of her school teachers. Her comradeship with her father began early in life and was continued to the time of his death. The family came to the United States in 1841, making their home at first in Poughkeepsie, and afterwards in or near Wappinger's Falls, where the father bought a large building-lot and erected a neat and commodious house, which remained in the possession of the family until sold by Mrs. Cunningham after the death of her husband. The lot was soon converted into a garden by its owner who tilled it with the spade and allowed no plough to be used in his little Eden. It was characteristic of his generous spirit, too, that none of the surplus product was ever sold, but was freely given to less favored neighbors. Happy years were spent by Mr. Cunningham in his shop, in his garden, with his books, and in visiting his daughter Jennie in New York after her marriage when she became established there. It was as nearly an ideal life as a modest man could desire. He lived respected by the best people in the community, and died in peace, with his children around him.

As I remember my sister in early life, the sunniness of her nature is the first and prevailing characteristic that I call to mind; occasional moods of reverie bordering on melancholy only made brighter the habitual radiance and buoyancy of a nature that diffused happiness all around her. She was a perfectly healthy girl in mind and body. A sound mind in a sound body was her noble heritage. She was always extremely temperate in food and drink, fastidious in all her tastes and personal habits, indulgent never beyond the dictates of perfect simplicity and sobriety. Proficient in all branches of housekeeping, her apparel was mostly of her own making. Good literature was a passion with her, and while never an omnivorous reader, she had a natural instinct for the best in language. A spirit of indomitable independence, courage and persistence in purpose characterized her from childhood. She must think her own thoughts, and mark out and follow her own path. Suffering from a degree of physical timidity that at times caused her much pain, she possessed a spirit that sometimes seemed to border on audacity in the assertion and maintenance of her own convictions. From childhood she developed a personality which charmed all with whom she came in contact. Persons of both sexes, young and old, the sober and the gay, alike fell under the influence of her magnetic power. Living for a time in the family of her brother, to whom she proffered her services as housekeeper when he was pastor of a Union church in Worcester County, Mass., she drew to her all sorts of people by the brightness and charm of her personality. Self-forgetful and genuine, interested in all about her, she lived only to serve others, valuing lightly all that she did. Here it was that her remarkable capacity for journalism first developed itself. One of the means by which she interested the community was the public reading of a semi-monthly paper, every line of which was written by herself and a fellow worker. The reading of that paper every fortnight, to an audience that crowded the church, was an event in her history.

Jennie was no dreamer. She was no speculative theorist spinning impossible things out of the cobwebs of her brain. She was no Hypatia striving to restore the gods of the past, revelling in a brilliant cloudland of symbolisms and affinities. If she was caught in the mist at any time, she soon came out of it and found her footing in the practical realities of daily life. Never over-reverential, she never called in question the deeper realities of soul-life. She was no ascetic: she would have made a poor nun. But she was a born preacher if by preaching is meant the annunciation of a gospel to those who need it. Jennie was always an ardent devotee of her sex, and whatever else she believed in, she certainly believed in women, their instincts and capacities.

In the year 1856, on February 14th, St. Valentine's Day, my sister Jennie was married to David G. Croly, a reporter for the New York *Herald*, and they began life in the city on his meagre salary of fourteen dollars a week. The gifted young wife, however, soon found work for herself on the *World*, the *Tribune*, the *Times*, *Noah's Sunday Times* and the *Messenger*. The first money she received for writing was in return for an article published in the New York *Tribune*. Their joint career in metropolitan journalism was interrupted however by a short term of residence in Rockford, Illinois, where Mr. Croly was invited to become editor of the Rockford *Register*, then owned by

William Gore King, the husband of our sister
Mary A. Cunningham. Mr. Croly was aided in
the editorial management by his wife, and while
the work was agreeable and successful, it was due
to Mrs. Croly's ardent desire for a larger field,
that at the end of a year they decided to return to
New York. The results for both abundantly
justified the change. As managing editor of the
daily *World* for a number of years, afterwards of
the New York *Graphic*, and later of the *Real
Estate Record and Guide*, Mr. Croly won an honorable position in New York journalism. He
was a conservative democrat of the strictest
sort, a radical in religion, and .had but little
appreciation of the deeper forces at work in society and in national life. But he was able and
honest, and enjoyed the respect of his fellow-
craftsmen.

"Jenny June" was a person of very different
mental and moral mould. Her work soon revealed
a new, fresh, vigorous force in journalism. An
examination of her editorial contributions to the
Sunday Times from March to December, 1861,
suggests her mental vivacity, vigor, breadth of
view, and uniform clearness and power of expression. The title of the whole series is unpretentious
enough: "Parlor and Sidewalk Gossip." All
through her journalistic career similar qualities
of originality characterized her pen. She was
editor of *Demorest's* magazine for twenty-seven

years, and was both editor and owner of *Godey's* magazine and *The Home-Maker*. *The Cycle* was her own creation and property. In each of these publications the dominating thoughts are those which make for social elevation, the honor of womanhood and home comfort and happiness. In addition to this editorial work she was a regular contributor to several leading newspapers in Boston, Chicago, New Orleans, Baltimore and other cities. She inaugurated the system of syndicate correspondence, and was the author of several books—" For Better, For Worse "; " Talks on Women's Topics "; " Thrown on Her Own Resources"; three manuals; and " The History of the Woman's Club Movement," a large volume of nearly twelve hundred pages.

During the most active years of my sister's literary life, she had also the care of a large household, and her home was always bright and hospitable. The Croly Sunday evening receptions were one of the social features of New York City.

Five children were born to Mr. and Mrs. Croly. Minnie, the eldest, was happily married to Lieutenant Roper of the U. S. Navy; her early death was a grief hard to bear. The second child, a boy, died in infancy. The surviving children are: Herbert G. Croly, a man of letters in New York City; Vida Croly Sidney, the wife of the English playwright, Frederick Sidney, lives in London;

and Alice Cary Mathot, the wife of a New York lawyer, William F. Mathot, resides in Brooklyn Hills, Long Island.

Mrs. Croly, one of the founders of Sorosis, perhaps the most noted woman's club in existence, was its President for many years, and its Honorary President at the time of her death. The cause which led to the founding of Sorosis is an open secret. Women were ignored at the Charles Dickens reception; this was not to be tolerated, and in consequence of this affront Sorosis came into being, an effectual protest against any similar indifference in all time to come. Of the growth of the club movement in the United States, in Great Britain, France, Russia, and in far-off India, I do not propose to enter into detail. Suffice it to say that it is one of the marvels of the modern social and intellectual life of women.

What was the secret of Jenny June's charm and power? Not scholarship—let this be said in all sincerity. How greatly she appreciated the scholar's advantages was well known to her intimate friends. But these advantages did not belong to her. Nor did it consist in inherited social rank or wealth; her earnings by her pen were large, but her patrimony was small. It should have been said before, that she received the degree of Doctor of Literature from Rutgers Women's College, and was appointed to a new chair of Journalism and Literature in that institution.

She was also a lecturer in other women's schools of the first rank.

Nor did Jenny June pattern her work according to the advice or after the example of any one man or woman. There was no example by which she could be guided. Woman was a new factor in journalism, and Jenny June was a new woman, a new creation, if I may so speak, fashioned after the type of woman in the beginning, when God created man and woman in His own image. I cannot too fully emphasize the fact that she was a new and original personality in journalism. No one understood this better than her husband. In matters of detail his counsel was of value to her, but the spirit and character of her work were her own; and happily for her and for womankind she could never be diverted from her chosen path. This, indeed, was one chief secret of her success. She was unalterably true to her divine womanly ideals of woman's nature, place in society and redemptive work. I say redemptive work, for it was one of her deepest convictions that woman's function was to be the saving salt of all life. Sorosis was founded upon this idea;—not a literary club merely or mainly; not a political, social or religious club; but one founded on womanhood, on the divine nature of women of every class and degree.

Jenny June's recognition of this vital truth brought her into sympathy with a world-wide movement. The new woman is no monstrosity, no sporadic creature born of intellectual fermentation and unrest, but the rise and development of a better, nobler type of womanhood the world over. Jenny June's eminent distinction was that she was a leader in this movement. It made her what her husband once said in my hearing: "a wonderful woman." Of course there was the capacity for bursts of feeling on occasion, which those who knew her best seldom cared to provoke. "I am not an amiable woman," she once said to the writer. Radiant as she was, there was a volcanic force in her nature which could be terrific against folly, frivolity and wrong.

Thousands of gifted women are now making themselves heard in poetry, dissertation, fiction and journalism because Jenny June opened the path for them. Womanhood was her watchword, and God, duty, faith and hope the springs of her life. It may surprise even those who knew her well to learn that her physical timidity was great, and at times painful. But her moral and intellectual courage impelled her at times almost to the verge of audacity, and was held under restraint only by conscience and good sense. Humor and wit can hardly be said to have been marked traits in her mentality. There was something delphic and oracular often in her familiar conversation. Sentimentalism had no place in her nature, her reading or literary work. A soul full of healthy and noble sentiment left no room for sentiment-alism.

Was Jenny June a genius? Well, if a boundless capacity for good original work is genius, then she was a genius. Magnanimity was a marked trait in her character. Envy or jealousy of the gifts of another were foreign to her. Love of nature, and especially of fine trees, was one of her most noticeable characteristics. "There will be trees in my heaven," she once said to the writer. But works of art, of the chisel, the brush, the pencil and the loom were her delight. She loved the city, its crowding humanity, its stores and its galleries. She loved London even more than New York. Continental travel was her chief pleasure and diversion. A long period of physical suffering, caused by an accident, cast a cloud over the last years of my sister's honorable life. She sought relief from pain and weakness, at Ambleside in Derbyshire, England, and at a celebrated cure in Switzerland, but was only partially successful. The final release came on December 23, 1901, and her remains were laid by the side of her husband in the cemetery at Lakewood, New Jersey.

Noble Jenny June! Shall we ever see her like again!

Sorosis-Press Club Memorial Meeting

A MEMORIAL meeting, called by Sorosis jointly with the Woman's Press Club, was held at the Waldorf-Astoria on January 6, 1902, a fortnight after the death of Mrs. Croly. It was attended not alone by the members of these two clubs but also by representatives from every woman's club in New York and the vicinity. Letters from many clubs belonging to the General Federation were read, and from the secretary's report of the meeting have been gathered the following tributes of notable clubwomen to the beloved founder of both clubs.

Address by Dimies T. S. Denison, President of Sorosis

WE have met this afternoon to pay a loving tribute to one of the departed of Sorosis, who was for many years its President, and for years its Honorary President.

The loss is not ours alone, for our sorrow is shared by all clubwomen, from Australia around the world to Alaska. Her position will always remain unique. Whenever there comes a time for a great movement there has always been a leader. The Revolution had its Washington; the abolition of slavery its Lincoln; and so, when the time came for such a movement among women, there were also leaders. Mrs. Croly remained, throughout her life, an advocate of everything which was for the betterment of women, and she died in the heart of the movement.

Her perception of the value of unity, of the advantage of organized effort, was remarkable. Perhaps the generations beyond ours will think of her most in that quality, but the women of our time will remember her, as they loved her, for her ready sympathy and her unfailing helpfulness to all women. Though departed, she is still with

15

us, and the beauty of her life remains, in that its influence is imperative.

Mrs. Croly had that particular sense of fellow-ship among women most unusual. If you will stop to think, in our language you will find that there are no words to express that thought, except those that are masculine — fellowship, brother-hood, fraternity. Mrs. Croly, perhaps more than any other woman in the world, had the sense of what fellowship or fraternity meant in women, and although she sometimes may have been called an idealist or sentimentalist, it is recognized by many women that this thought must be abiding, for in a federation it is the spirit that is current through it that keeps the federation alive.

The last afternoon it was my privilege to be with Mrs. Croly we had a long talk, and it seems to me, in looking back, that Mrs. Croly was then leaving a message with me for all clubwomen. I never heard her speak so eloquently. We talked of some of the problems of the General Federation —its possible disruption. Mrs. Croly said: "It does not matter; if anything happens that the General Federation should be disrupted, another will be formed at once." She had absolute faith, if not in a Divine Providence, that there was a possibility it was part of the human scheme of development that must be carried on through the Divine Will. So, if she left any message for the General Federation, it was this: that whatever

MRS. CROLY
at the age of 40.
(About the time Sorosis was inaugurated.)

our personal opinions are, whatever we think of any question, we are to think first of the life of the General Federation; because in it is the great thought of the fellowship and fraternity among women that is to bring us closer and closer to the millennium.

Address by Charlotte B. Wilbour

WHEN a soul that has worn out its frail body in the work of the world crosses the threshold of eternity, the darkness that gathers around our hearts has in it a relief of light. Nature has suffered no violence; the power of the body has been exhausted in good service, and the tired spirit is set free from the encasement that can no longer serve it. A fond look backward, a hopeful look forward, and the portals close with our benediction.

> " A life that dares send
> A challenge to the end,
> And, when it comes, say
> ' Welcome, friend,' "

inspires the wish that we may so fill the measure of our days with usefulness.

The departure of such a spirit would be fittingly commemorated by the grand marches of Chopin and Beethoven, or the majestic requiems of Mozart, rather than by our simple words. And yet they are our hearts' testimony to her in whose name we are assembled and, let us hope, made worthy. To us who believe that life reels not back from the white charger of Death towards the

gulf of inanity and oblivion, there is a vivid realization that our words may be spoken to the conscious spirit; and we desire that, in the sacred
name of truth, and with the love that comprehends
and overcomes, we may speak simply as "soul to
soul."

One of the most beautiful lessons I have learned
of death is that after the departure of a friend, or
even of an acquaintance, our memories retain and
cherish their best and noblest qualities and deeds.
We repeat their finest words and recount their
generous works. The sunshine falls clear on
their virtues, and the shadow lies kindly on their
faults. It exalts our nature that our minds elect
only the lovely and beautiful characteristics of the
lost friend. This sublime power in us breaks the
force of the bitter criticism of the obituary, the eul-
ogy, and the epitaph—that they are false notes
in a hymn of praise. And to us yet living, there
is sweet comfort in the thought that our best and
higher selves shall remain with those we love and
honor. And so shall the good we do live after us.
These purified remembrances are links of the chain
that binds the humblest to the highest.

In my early womanhood I knew our honored
president, a fair, happy, healthy, active English
woman; and she appeared to me (sobered by the
loss of most of my family) to rejoice in a fulness
of life. We were maidens, and her interests
and activities were in domestic and social life. I

have not lost the fresh memory of her in those days.

She was our president for ten years, and afterwards our honorary president. The activity of her life has made the deepest impression upon me. Every member of our association and of sister associations will agree with me, that never a woman brought a more cheerful and willing spirit to her official duties than did she. She rejoiced in her place, delighted in her privilege, and fully enjoyed the recognition and good fellowship of other clubs. This cheerful service, rendered for years, made her widely known in the club world. She responded to personal influence and suggestions made directly to her. She was most receptive to practical ideas, and adopted methods readily, and her liberal service brought to her just recompense.

For years it required sacrifice on her part to attend the regular meetings of Sorosis, for she had daily occupation, and a lost day must be redeemed. But when an officer she made the sacrifice cheerfully. She was social and hospitable. Freely her house was given to us for lectures, receptions to distinguished guests and business meetings. For years the Positivists held their meetings at her home. She found her pleasure in pleasing, and in helping others gave herself joy. She loved her work for clubs, and you will remember that she had several business enterprises connected

with them, during the years that she was an
active clubwoman.

I was in this country while she was preparing
her history of clubs (not the history of Sorosis),
and she brought the interest and enthusiasm of a
young woman to the work; with a satisfied pride
she showed me the material she had collected for
the history.   Nothing else to her mind was more
important, or to be thought of until that was accomplished.   I believe that her usefulness to clubs
has been commensurate with the interest and
gratification she had in the service.

During the years of our acquaintance our intercourse was genial and concordant, and the results
of our early work in Sorosis cannot equal the
sweet satisfaction that came with its performance.

In the early life of the club many of us were
young mothers, and our domestic duties had
strong claims upon us, and one prominent thought
in connection with the formation of Sorosis was
that the attention of a large class of thinking
women, directed in concert towards important domestic and social questions, could be secured; and,
while the character of the club should be pre-emi-
nently social, we hoped to quietly bring in important reforms, or at least some effective action on
these questions, and, above all, to secure an intelligent social intercourse without increasing our
domestic duties and responsibilities.   Have we not
accomplished this?

As the smallest consoling thought is greater than the most eloquent expression of sorrow, so do we find some consolation in the fact that fate was kind to our friend, and led her away when she could no longer enjoy life, and that she went while with us whose hearts were warm with an active sympathy and tender helpfulness.

Our kind purpose to her name lifts our acts above criticism, and fortifies them by our love and worthiness of intention. Let us live to live for-ever—so shall we never fear death; let our warm human love be the prophet of a union for greater benefits; and let us have faith in the love that lives in human bosoms still:

> "Lives to renovate our earth
> From the bondage of its birth,
> And the long arrears of ill."

Address by the Rev. Phebe A. Hanaford
Vice-President of the Woman's Press
Club of New York City

I AM requested to speak of the excellent work done by its departed president, in and for the Woman's Press Club of New York City. To others is assigned the testimony in reference to the career and work of our departed president as a press woman, and her place in literature.

We are not here to analyze her character, or to chronicle her work. Nor are we here to dwell on those biographical details which belong to the pen rather than the voice; to the book and the reader rather than the address and the hearer. We are here to testify our regard for one whose busy pen is laid aside, but whose example of industry we may well imitate; though in the journalistic field the women of to-day will never have opportunity to emulate her perseverance and fearlessness, since her entrance in times long gone by on this untrodden path bore an important part in opening the way and obtaining results for women with whom the pen to-day is a power.

Mrs. Croly was the founder of this club in 1889, and for twelve years and to the day of her death, its only president. It started (as she tells us in the large quarto volume relating to clubs—which was the closing, if not the crowning, effort of her busy pen) with an invitation sent out by herself in November, 1889, to forty women, a number of whom were then engaged upon the press in New York City, to meet at her residence, and consider the advisability of forming a Woman's Press Club. It was eminently fitting that one who had been stirred in former years by the absence of social recognition in journalism as within woman's province, on the part of the men of the press, and moved to take a prominent part in the formation of Sorosis, should organize a club of women writers — women journalists especially — which should be known everywhere as distinctly a Woman's Press Club.

The response to her call was most gratifying. Her ability as an organizer, and her social qualities which could attract and hold women together in strong bonds of mutual esteem and fellowship, were again evident, and on November 19, 1889, the organization was effected and a provisional constitution adopted.

At first the literary features of the new club were considered secondary to the social and beneficiary, but gradually they grew to their present importance.

In its early days, like most clubs this one was migratory, and its work incidental. Gradually it

came to have a more permanent home, and its
monthly programmes which, as Mrs. Croly herself
stated, "are more in the form of a symposium than
of a question for debate," came to be so attractive
and varied, and in every way so excellent, that
they are often declared to be unsurpassed in interest by any woman's club. This was a matter
of exceeding satisfaction to its founder, who saw
the club grow from its membership of fifty-two
to two hundred. She was never weary of re-
counting its successes, literary, musical, artistic
and social. The Press Club was her joy and pride
from its organization to the very day when she
last met with its members, devoting on that day
her failing strength to a cause that was beyond
expression dear to her heart. I think I shall only
be saying very feebly what the members of the
club, especially those who have been members
from its organization, now feel—that they regard
her presence with them on the recent day of in-
stallation of new officers as a benediction, though
they little knew that in her feebleness she was
bidding them a loving farewell. When the news
of her departure reached them it was received with
surprise and deep sorrow. By prompt action the
officers at once came together, and immediate
measures were taken for appropriate expression
of the Press Club's loyalty and love.

Its members are here to-day not only to express
their own high regard for their departed founder

and president, but also to unite with Sorosis, the London Pioneer Club, and other clubs in the State Federation, who, by their presence, speech, or song, indicate the sympathy they have with those who will hold in fadeless remembrance their ascended president, who has learned ere this, that

> "Life is ever Lord of Death,
> And Love can never lose its own."

As members of the club she, who has now passed into the eternal light, founded may we seek earnestly to walk in the light of Truth, strenuous for that more than royal liberty of conscience, which means liberty under righteous law and seeking for the Unity which obeys the Golden Rule, and thus binds heart to heart. So shall the Woman's Press Club of New York City truly honor the memory of its founder and first president, Jane Cunningham Croly.

Address by Orlena A. Zabriskie, President of the New York Federation

THAT the New York State Federation should be called upon to attest its love, devotion, and admiration for Mrs. Croly and her wonderful work among women, is a privilege we appreciate, and I shall try in a few simple, honest words, to explain a little of what her influence has been to the New York State Federation. We all know she was an organizer and founder, but it is well to repeat those words, although I think there is little danger that we shall ever forget them. From all over the State have come messages to me from different members of the federation, expressing their love and obligation to Mrs. Croly for what she has done for them individually, and for the State. One letter said:

"I shall think of her always as that lovely, sweet-tempered woman who, under the most trying circumstances, never lost her temper, or felt she was at all aggrieved. She took it in the right way, and was just as lovely and kind at the close as at the beginning."

I saw her at Friendship, a little town in the northwestern part of the State, before the meeting at Buffalo, and there we had a long talk about

27

matters of Federation interest. She gave me some
good advice in her own gentle way, that I shall
never forget, and I am only too glad to have this
opportunity of saying it helped me to carry through
that convention as I could not have done otherwise.

What was the secret of her power as an organizer? I think this—she saw the little spark of
good in each woman, every woman she came in
contact with, and even in those she did not come
in personal contact with. She knew it was there
and she had the ability to call it forth, and that
magnetic influence drew them together, so that
they realized that they could do more in large
numbers than they could as individuals. Knowing our power, she urged and encouraged us to do
our best. When with her we did not feel as
though we had a " specked " side. I think it
was just that that gave her power and influence in
the clubs she founded, to make them live and be
a greater power than ever they could have been
without her memory and example set before them.

She has done good work, and started us on a
task that she saw had practical possibilities, and
now we can carry out those ideas of hers, and
give them force in years to come. It may take a
long time, but we will keep on being patient,
cheerful, kind-hearted, and considerate, as she
was. Let us therefore be grateful we had her
as long as we did. She was for us a grand inheritance, and let us appreciate it.

Address by Carrie Louise Griffin, President of the Society of American Women in London

IF I could only command that physical self as I would like to, I would tell you how grateful I am to be privileged to speak, and how much I think we have to be thankful for to-day, in the life of our dear one, which was given us.

I am new in this club, and, as most of you know, my friendship with Mrs. Croly is not yet three years old, but I have been singularly privileged and honored in loving her, and in the love which she gave me.

She came into my life (I must be just a little personal for a moment) as our first luncheon, in our little Society of American Women in London, was about to be given. The president of Sorosis had written to London saying: "Do you know that Mrs. Croly and Mrs. Glynes are to be in London, and I think they would help you?" Bless her, and Mrs. Croly: she came as a benediction to the few of us who were then novices in what we were doing. I can never tell you what a benefit she was to us in the difficult work we had undertaken. You have given me exceptional privileges

in coming among you, and I am grateful for the
help you have been to me, but I would say to you
—and you have given me this privilege—I have
never met a woman who seemed to have recognized the birthright in women as the birthright
in men, to create that link which binds our powers
to our intellect.   It seems to me that it was with
Mrs. Croly as it was with our late Majesty,
Queen Victoria, that she was an influence, perhaps, rather than a power.   She conceived great
ideas and passed them on for the executive work
of others to fulfil.   I can assure you she was
everything to us.   Her English birth gave her an
instinctive insight into English character.   English women seemed to know and understand her,
as she knew and understood them, and there has
been no finer link between the women of America
and the women of the Old World than Mrs.
Croly.   It was my privilege to be with her personally a great deal while in London, not only when
she stayed in my own house, but when I have
gone back and forth with her as her guide to the
many functions we attended together.   We can
all be proud of her.   Wherever she went she was
not only hailed as the pioneer woman, but also
as one who did honor and credit to the name of
American womanhood, for, although born in
England, she still claimed that she was an
American woman, as you know.

I shall never forget a little picture she gave of

herself one day. She told us of her life in her
home in a little town in the north of England.
Her father was a Unitarian, and often had classes
in his house for teaching the working people.
His views, as you may imagine, were quite con-
trary to the views of the orthodox Church of England, and the people there rebelled, stoned the
house, and wanted to turn them out of the town.
The mother said to the father: "I wish you would
take little Jennie by the hand, in her white frock,
and lead her out to the people; perhaps when
they see her they will not throw stones." That
was her earliest memory of that little English
town. Later, I believe, they left in the night and
came to America, in order that they might live
out the courage of their faith.

At our luncheon Mrs. Croly said: "I want
English and American women to love each other.
I remember with pride and honor my English
birth. I can see my little room now—a small
room with a lattice window over which the roses
grew, and as I stood at the window on tiptoe, I
could look into the old-fashioned garden below.
I stood on an old chest. In the winter my summer frocks were kept there, and in the summer
my red woollen dress. I loved it; it was beautiful, and it made me love England. When I am
in England and I hear anything not quite kind
about America, I am sorry and my heart aches,
and if, when I am in America, I hear something

not quite kind about England, my heart aches again, because I love it all."

In talking with Mrs. Croly, she said to me, " I hope some day you will come to a General Federation." Quoting Matthew Arnold, she said: " If ever the world sees a time when women shall come together, purely and simply for the benefit and good of mankind, it will be a power such as the world has never known." And she said, " There you will find it." We had talked about it and looked forward to seeing it together, but that will never be. It was her hope and dream that there should be such a General Federation of clubs as to bring in the women of the Old World with the Federation of Clubs in the New, that we might stand hand in hand together. She said to me, " I think you are narrow in your society—its members are only Americans." We have often talked this over, and have decided that in order to strengthen our centre we must keep it, at present, to American woman; but it may be possible to have an associate membership—the thin edge of the wedge looking toward the realization of her dreams.

Address by Cynthia Westover Alden, Vice-
President of the Women's Press Club,
and President of the International Sunshine Society

MRS. CROLY has left us. Yet I cannot think of
her work as ended, of her mission as closed. You
may go over every line she ever wrote, you may
recall with microscopic exactness every word she
ever spoke, without finding one single grain of
bitterness towards any human creature. Her active life was such as must find the ripe continuance of its activity in the better country whither
she has preceded us. I feel that there is no hy-
perbole in applying to her memory the striking
words of Lowell's Elegy on Dr. Channing:

"I do not come to weep above thy pall
    And mourn the dying-out of noble powers;
The poet's clearer eye should see in all
    Earth's seeming woe, seed of immortal flowers.

"No power can die that ever wrought for truth;
    Thereby a law of Nature it became,
And lives unwithered in its blithesome youth,
    When he who called it forth is but a name.

3

"Therefore I cannot think thee wholly gone;
  The better part of thee is with us still;
Thy soul its hampering clay aside hath thrown,
  And only freer wrestles with the ill.

"Thou art not idle; in thy higher sphere
  Thy spirit bends itself to loving tasks,
And strength to perfect what it dreamed of here
  Is all the crown and glory that it asks."

The women of America owe much to Jenny June. By example she showed them that the career of letters was open to them. Her style, cheerful and vivid, sometimes epigrammatic, always entertaining, was her own. It could not be copied, it could not be imitated, it stood by itself; her career, filled with a large measure of the courage of her success, belonged in the broadest sense to women as women. How many worthy ambitions that career has stimulated to fruition we know not, and never shall know. One thing, however, is certain—that if you deduct from the literature of America the names of women who have followed Mrs. Croly's example and have been cheered by the fact that she did not fall by the wayside, you leave a void that never could be filled. How consciously they have been affected by Mrs. Croly's blazing path I cannot tell; but the influence has been none the less real and none the less powerful.

Woman's battle for literary recognition will not have to be fought over again: it belongs to the past. The old contempt of editors and publishers, aye, and of readers as well, has gone to join slavery and polygamy and human sacrifices in the chamber of horrors. But we can never forget the woman who braved that contempt, and faced it down by achievement that could not be ignored. Mrs. Croly belonged to the period of that early struggle. In her sweetness of temper she lent to its very asperities the charm of a tournament, overcoming evil with good, and triumphing at last over prejudice which thousands of women had feared to face. We loved her for herself. We are sad in spite of ourselves that she has gone. But we shall only remember her as one of the greatest benefactors of woman in literature; one of the most delightful of all the delightful characters that we have ever known.

"This laurel leaf I cast upon thy bier;
   Let worthier hands than these thy wreath entwine;
Upon thy hearse I shed no useless tear—
   For us weep rather thou, in calm divine."

In the Silence

By May Riley Smith

THEY are out of the chaos of living,
   The wreck and debris of the years;
They have passed from the struggle and striving,
   They have drained their goblet of tears.
They have ceased one by one from their labors,
   So we clothed them in garments of rest,
And they entered the chamber of silence;—
   God do for them now what is best!

We saw not the lift of the curtain,
   Nor heard the invisible door,
As they passed where life's problems uncertain
   Will follow and burthen no more.
We lingered and wept on the threshold—
   The threshold each mortal must cross,—
Then we laid a new wreath down upon it,
   To mark a new sorrow and loss.

Then back to our separate places
   A little more lonely we creep,
A little more care in our faces,
   The wrinkles a little more deep.
And we stagger, ah, God, how we stagger

As we lift the old load to our back!
A little more lonely to carry
  Because of the comrade we lack.

But into our lives whether chidden
  Or welcome, God's comforters come;
His sunshine waits not to be bidden,
  His stars,—they are always at home.
His mornings are faithful,—His evenings
  Allay the day's fever and fret;
And night—kind physician—entreats us
  To slumber and dream and forget.

O Spirit of infinite kindness
  And gentleness passing all speech!
Forgive when we miss in our blindness
  The comforting hand thou dost reach.
Thou sendest the Spring on Thine errand
  To soften the grief of the world;
For us is the calm of the mountain,
  For us is the rose-leaf uncurled.

Thou art tenderer, too, than a mother,
  In the wonderful Book it is said;
O Pillow of Comfort!   What other
  So softly could cradle my head?
And though Thou hast darkened the portal
  That leads where our vanished ones be;
We lean on our faith in Thy goodness,
  And leave them to silence and Thee.

Jenny June

By Fanny Hallock Carpenter

A BEAUTIFUL soul has journeyed
   Out from the Now into Then.
Her voice echoes back to us, waiting,
   The sound of the great Amen.

Her life was a song so winsome
   It sung itself night and day
Into the hearts of the people
   Who met her along the way.

Her life was a flower so fragrant
   That every one passing her, knew
By the perfume from it exhaling,
   The love out of which it grew.

Her life was a book so vivid
   That all, though running, could read
The story of earnest endeavor
   Written for woman's need.

Her life was a light whose radiance
   Brightened all woman-kind,
As sunshine wakens the flowers,
   Or genius illumines the mind.

Her life was a poem so tender
  It thrilled with its cadence sweet
Many a life prosaic,
  Which caught up the rhythmic beat.

Her life was a bell whose ringing
  Gave no uncertain sound,
Its chiming rang out to the nations
  And girdled the world around.

Her life was a deed so holy,
  So noble, so brave, so true,
That it set all womanhood noting
  The good one woman could do.

Her life was a brook, that swelling
  Grew to a river wide,
That freshened the souls of the many
  Touched by its flowing tide.

The song has trilled into silence,
  The flower is faded and gone,
The book's strong story is ended,
  The light is lost in the dawn.

The poem's sweet rhythm is ended,
  The chiming has ceased to be,
The deed is fully accomplished,
  The river has joined the sea.

She dropped the pebble whose ripples
    To the shores of all time shall extend,
She has spoken the word into ether
    Whose sound-waves never shall end.

She has started a light on its journey
    Out into limitless space,
She has written a thought for women
    Eternity cannot erase.

A wonderful soul has journeyed
    Out from the Now into Then,
Her voice echoes back to us, waiting,
    The sound of the great Amen.

Resolutions and Tributes
From Clubs

Woman's Press Club
(of New York City)

January eleventh, 1902

At a meeting of the Club held this day the following resolutions were unanimously adopted:

Whereas, Mrs. Jennie Cunningham Croly (Jennie June), our dearly beloved Founder and President, has been taken from us by death, after service as President covering an unbroken period of thirteen years, and

Whereas, During this period, and previous to this, she won our admiration, esteem and deep affection by her inspired efforts and untiring energy in behalf of women, her high intellectual powers, and her charm of character, now therefore, be it

Resolved, That we, the members of the Woman's Press Club of New York City, record this minute upon our records as a lasting reminder of her achievements. And be it further

Resolved, That a copy of these resolutions be forwarded to the family of our deceased Founder and President, as showing our profound sorrow for the loss to the whole world of a woman of extraordinary mind and heart, a writer of great talent, and a Christian gentlewoman.

Miriam Mason Greeley

Margaret W. Ravenhill.

Harriet Holt Dey

Cynthia Westover Alden

Phebe A. Hanaford,
President

Elizabeth B. Brenton
Recording Secretary

Caroline M. Morse
Chairman Memorial Committee

Fac-simile of resolu   an's Press Club of

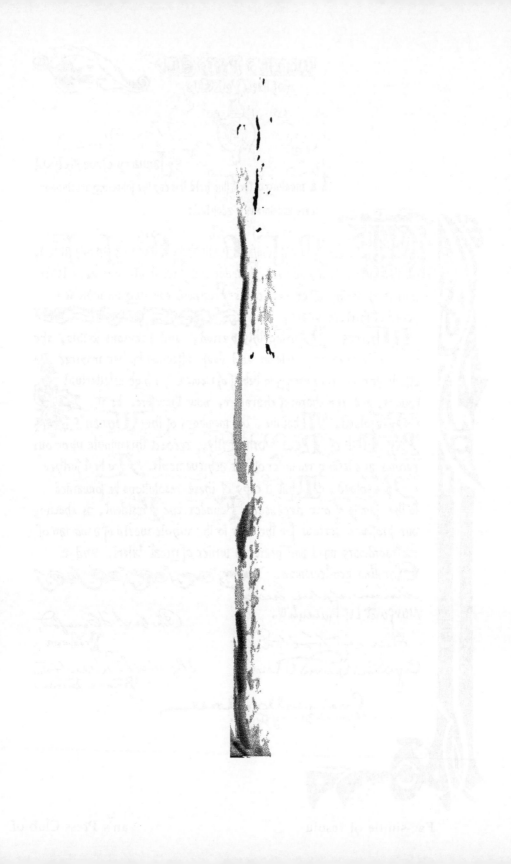

Resolutions of the New York State Federation of Women's Clubs

In Memoriam

Mrs. Jane Cunningham Croly

WE have tenderly laid away to rest our beloved honorary president, Jane Cunningham Croly, to sleep the blessed sleep that knows no waking in this toilsome, troublous world.

Her gentle soul is at peace, her personal work is accomplished, her useful life is ended. She has been taken from further pain and further labor, to that existence where all is perfect peace, perfect rest, perfect rhythm.

We wish to place upon our records, therefore, our appreciation of the fact, that this New York State Federation of Women's Clubs has suffered such a loss as can come but once to any, a loss like that of a loving mother to an affectionate child.

We shall miss her at our meetings, at our larger gatherings, and at our conventions.

We shall hold her, and the desires of her heart in relation to us, in loving and constant memory.

And we purpose to take up her work, where she laid it down, and carry it on with the same unselfish aims, high ideals, and unremitting patience with which she labored, until we shall reach the goal upon which her farseeing eyes were fastened, and her great heart was set.

FANNY HALLOCK CARPENTER.

February 13, 1902.

The Society of American Women in Lond

At a Meeting of this Society held at their
Prince's Piccadilly, London, on Monday, the 24th
March, 1902:

It was unanimously Resolved as follows:—

That the Members of this Society
with deep regret the death of their first
Member, Mrs Jennie Cunningham Croly,
as a pioneer Woman Journalist, and pioneer C
Woman, helped to establish ideals of usefu
for Women new to her time.

That this Society, in regarding her life, fee
that a debt of gratitude is due to her, for
unfailing faith in womankind; her asp
for their unity; her hope for their advancemen
and for her work for women's organizations wh
declared objects are to make the world wiser
better

Resolutions adopted by The Society of American Women in London,
March 24th, 1902.

By the founding of Sorosis, an example was set, a symbol of unity was established.

The cause she espoused, in the early days of doubt and difficulty, has now acquired power and importance, and bids fair to accomplish greater results than even she, its most sanguine supporter, imagined.

She builded better than she knew; as do all who build by faith.

In the plenitude of the harvest let us not forget the Sower of seed.

Let us remember with thankfulness her steadfast endeavours, and by trying to realize the ideals she laboured for, let us ever keep her memory green.

a copy of these resolutions be engrossed and to the members of the family, and to Sorosis

ned)

Ella M. Dietz Glynes,
Acting President.

May Tifft Fay,
Chairman of Executive Committee.

L. B. Temple Kett
Corresponding Secretary,

The Members
of the
Special
Committee

The Croly Memorial Fund of the Pioneer Club of London

First Annual Report

In July, 1900, a fund was raised by the exertions of Mrs. E. S. Willard, to present a life membership of the Pioneer Club to Mrs. Jane Cunningham Croly, known to all who are interested in woman's work as " Jenny June."

Mrs. Croly had a special claim to this distinction, for she was the originator of women's clubs. The first woman's club was founded by her in New York, March, 1868, under the name of " Sorosis." The example was quickly followed elsewhere, and when, in 1889, Sorosis, to celebrate its majority, called a convention of women's clubs, ninety-seven were known to exist in the United States. This convention led to a Federation with biennial meetings. In 1896, the Federation included one thousand four hundred and twenty-five clubs. The Pioneer is the only English woman's club which belongs to the Federation.

Mrs. Croly's activities were not confined to clubs, although up to the time of her death the movement owed much to her wisdom and energy. She was a journalist, a writer, an admirable critic,

and all her life a devoted worker for every movement that could raise the position of women.

She was a dear and valued friend of Mrs. Mar-
singberd, the president and founder of this club.
It was a recognition of their unity of spirit and
purpose that made the response of this club so
ready that the only life-membership as yet presented, was offered to Mrs. Croly. She was
deeply gratified, but unfortunately did not live
long enough to enjoy a privilege which she highly
esteemed. Her useful, loving, laborious life ended
in December, 1901. But she had been among
us from time to time. Her interest in us never
flagged, and we prize some tokens of her regard.
Nor shall we soon forget the stirring words she
addressed to us on two occasions, pointing out the
opportunities which our association gave for useful work and sympathy.

When the life-membership fee had been paid,
some money still remained, and when the question arose as to what should be done with it, Lady
Hamilton made the valuable suggestion that it
should be used as the foundation of a fund to be
called "The Mrs. Croly Memorial Fund," to be
applied in sisterly loving kindness to such cases
as might arise within the club, where urgent
material help was needed. This suggestion was
heartily welcomed by a small provisional meeting
called by Mrs. E. S. Willard, October 15, 1902,
when preliminary steps were taken. At a second

meeting, November 25, a definite constitution was formed for the administration of the fund.

It is hoped that the members of the Pioneer Club will do all they can to support this fund, for it is an effort to give some tangible expression to the principles which governed the lives of both Mrs. Croly and our own president. They always unselfishly tried to give loving help to sister women.

January 27, 1903.

The Positivist Episode

The Positivist Episode

The Positivist Episode

By *Thaddeus B. Wakeman*

"The Positivist Episode was a positive factor in my life."—MRS. CROLY.

THOSE were bright, sunny, happy, idyllic, and fruitful days of the Positivist Episode, when the first of the two following letters which my wife and I now contribute to the "Memories of Mrs. Croly," were written. That episode, of which these letters represent the beginning, and the end throws an explaining light not only over the life of her whom this memorial is to honor, but over that of her husband, who passed to the higher life in 1889; and largely also over the lives of others more or less associated with, or affected by, the introduction of the study and culture of Positivism into America, of which they may be regarded as the chief promoters.

Yes, as friends of Mrs. Croly and of those dear to her, we may well recall, as she often did, this Positivist Episode as among the pleasantest of her —and may we not also add of ours?—earthly days. The first letter shows the movement well under way, when meetings had begun to be held, and visits to be made to the homes of those deeply interested.   Never shall we forget the first of those visits made by Mrs. Croly to our then "almost out of town" home in 116th street, where our house, pleasantly overlooking the East River, was clothed with trees and vines.   The Catawbas on a large trellis, trained in stories with upright canes, excited her admiration, and she assured us that she had "never seen nor eaten anybody's grapes with such delight."   Naturally, a basket or two of grapes soon followed to her home away down and over to the other side of town at number 19 Bank street.   Thus the "vines" and "fruit" referred to in her letter are explained; and with them was thus associated in holy sympathy her love with ours of "the kindly fruits of the earth."   Mr. Croly also referred to gifts of this kind in the New York *World*—thirty varieties of grapes raised under and in proof of the "law of correlation, expounded by the raiser as the law which held us of the world together."

But when our turn came as Positivist students to visit at their home, we found the cosey parlors well filled with the higher samples and fruits of human culture and intellect.   Mrs. Croly's social position, sustained by the ability of Mr. Croly and his prominence as managing editor of the New York *World*, and afterwards of the *Graphic*, enabled her to call together the leaders, and many interested in the then (and now?) two leading

schools of scientific and constructive thought; the
Positivist school of Auguste Comte, represented
by Henry Edgar and partly also by Mr. Croly and
others; and also in contrast therewith, the Syn-
thetic Philosophy of Herbert Spencer, represented
by Edward L. Youmans, John Fiske and others.
Nor were there wanting those who, like the present writer, would combine those two schools, and
more, into the scientific and republican growth of
our newer world and life in America.

The initiative of these meetings was a course of
lectures procured by Mr. Croly, to be delivered by
Mr. Edgar at De Garmo Hall early in 1868. Out
of the interest thus excited, Mr. and Mrs. Croly
called around them the elements above referred
to, including, among miscellaneous attendants,
perhaps a hundred earnest students of Positivism
and of the higher religious and scientific philoso-
phies. The meetings were not always held at the
homes mentioned, but at the home of Mr. Courtlandt Palmer and of other participants. All the
parties named, and many others, took part in the
discussions of this unorganized circle, until its
name and influence reached and interested generally the thinkers of the city. This interest, as
the years rolled on, resulted in or influenced the
forming of many societies, among which were a
Positivist Society, the Society of Humanity, the
New York and Manhattan Liberal Clubs, the
Philosophic Society of Brooklyn, the Nineteenth

Century Club, the Goethe Society, and indirectly
a Dante Society and several others. All of the
clubs and societies of women with which Mrs.
Croly and her work have been associated may be
thus included. Certain it is that this "positive
factor" in her life was the source from which the
new, altruistic inspiration originally came which
made her finally recognized as the "Mother of
Women's Clubs" and of their beneficent influences—the new life, light, and hope of women, of
which they are the beginning.

Nor less should be said for the literature that
has sprung from the same source. It began with
the "Positivist's Calendar," by Mr. Edgar, and
Professor Youmans's admirable collection of articles, and the introduction, on "Correlation" of
the physical and other forces, published by Apple-
ton, and never to be outgrown. Then Professor
Fiske published in the New York *World* his able
series of lectures on the "Positive Philosophy,"
which some think he weakened by turning into
the "Cosmic Philosophy." Then (for further
details are not in place here) Mr. and Mrs. Croly
and Mr. Bell and most of us went into literature
in some way, to an extent that made quite a li-
brary, now mostly lost or forgotten. Would that
I could "lend continuance to the time" of those
disputants, and show why and how they drifted
apart instead of together! For the shadow of
oblivion seems to be creeping over all; and against

that I, as the last survivor, seem to be their only and yet their helpless protector. Yet we can now see, as they mostly did not, that their divergence was really a " differentiation process," leading each to a higher integration of truth.

Thus, what I cannot do for each, the volunteer seeding of time is doing silently for all, though they noticed not the good seed they scattered. For instance, Mr. Croly wished these words to be placed over his grave: " I meant well, tried a little, failed much." He saw not that the sound seed of which he was a real and great sower, were his well-meant and effective efforts to bring Positivism, as the sum and synthesis of science and humanity, before all thoughtful American people, as the real religion and basis of their modern life. That view of life was then new, but now it is replacing or changing all dogmatic or supernatural religions. In a word, modern scientific thought is becoming practical, constructive, and positive in religion; directed more and more toward advantages in the human future on this earth. The real basis of sentiment is the new science of Sociology and the new sense of altruism—first named by Auguste Comte and first brought to the American people in and by this " Positivist Episode."

It is by the up-coming of such seed as was then sown, that the old issues and their old world have been replaced by the new; which we should gratefully inherit from those sowers. It is said that they seemed to look upon much of their life as failure because they did not see the harvest in their day as the direct result of their hands. How strange that the faith of evolution did not give them the "after sight" which is the crown and reward of those who "mean well," and who "work and hope!"

To Mrs. Croly did come not only the well-wishing and the patient labor, but also a foretaste of her reward. Her days were extended until her purposes fulfilled met the gratitude of her successors. Even "the slings and arrows of outrageous fortune," referred to in her last letter to us, were warded off by the human providence which, in her own words, "realizes the eternal goodness of the perfection of the order which governs the universe."

Thus her friendships with the many she loved and served have closed with unalloyed satisfaction—to me and mine a sincere friend for more than thirty years! And no words come that I might wish unsaid unless these: "Be careful now, for I have told more than one that you are my god-father!"

From Mrs. Croly to Mr. Wakeman

19 BANK STREET, NEW YORK,
Sept. 26, 1870.

MY DEAR MR. WAKEMAN:

Thank you very much for allowing us to share so largely in the luxuries of your pleasant home, and in the rewards of your labor. The grapes were a great treat to us, and we have enjoyed them exceedingly. The variety is wonderful; and the difference in the flavors, each one being perfect in itself, constantly excited our admiration.

I hope by this time your term of bachelorhood is at an end, and that Mrs. Wakeman and the children are with you. If she has arrived, please convey to her my acknowledgments for the card she left for me, and say how much I regretted not seeing her. Please also to remind her that next Monday (first Monday in October) is the meeting of Sorosis, and that I shall expect to find her at Delmonico's, corner of 14th street and Fifth avenue, at I P.M., as my guest. She can walk straight upstairs, and a waiter will send in her name to me, so that she need not enter alone; or she can arrive a little earlier (I am always there early) and see the ladies as they come.

As I have not many occasions for writing notes to you, Mr. Wakeman, I desire to say to you, with the deliberation with which one puts pen to paper, that I am thankful for having known so true a man, and happy that my husband can count him friend. One thing done is worth many words spoken, yet I am doubly glad when words and acts walk harmoniously together.

Always your obliged friend,

J. C. CROLY.

From Mrs. Croly to Mrs. Wakeman

7 BENTRICT TERRACE, REGENT'S PARK, N. W., LONDON, December 24, 1900.

MY DEAR OLD FRIEND:

I am sure that you have thought many times that I was forgetful and ungrateful, but indeed the first part of the indictment cannot be laid to my charge. I never forget you, and if I have not written, it is because I have suffered and enjoyed many things during the past two years, and have permanently lost the power of rapid movement, or of doing anything under great stress and pressure.

But now that this wonderful year is ending, this Sabbath of the centuries, I feel that I must at least send my love and unforgetness to you; also my hope that you are finding on the other side of the continent of North America, compensation for all that you left behind in the east, and greater promise for the future.

For all that I have gained for some years past I have to thank my losses. Chief among my gains is, I hope, a little realization of eternal goodness; of the perfection of the order which governs the universe, and the relation of every separate atom to the Divine Unity of the whole. I know Goethe proclaimed it a hundred years ago; but every separate part has to grow to its knowledge for itself.

I wonder how you are spending Christmas. This year seems to me so remarkable that it is a privilege to live in it. I am trying to use its last days as if they were mine, in doing the things I should be most sorry to leave undone.

I expect to return home soon—that is, in a few months. Or rather, as I have no home now, and a trustee has lost the money I had saved and entrusted to him in making provision for my old age, I shall only try to find a corner to rest in.

I hope you have been dealt with more kindly in body and estate. Please remember that I never forget the union of the spirit we once enjoyed— that the Positivist Episode was a positive factor in my life, and that I shall always recall Mr. Wakeman as my chief helper in it.

With love to you and yours, I am unforgettingly,

J. C. CROLY.

(It has seemed pertinent and interesting as bearing upon the "Positivist Episode" to here insert extracts from testimonials to Mr. Croly published in the memorial issued at the time of his death in May, 1889.)

From a Testimonial to Mr. Croly, by T. B. Wakeman

David G. Croly must not be forgotten. He rendered our country an invaluable service, not yet recognized. He was the man who *planted Positivism in America.* The many who have felt, the thousands who hereafter will feel its influence for good, should learn to bless, and to teach others to bless and continue his memory and influence.

In 1867–68 he began his great work. Henry Edgar had the seed from Comte direct, and then tried to sow it in a course of lectures given in a hall chiefly paid for by Mr. Croly. But the seed would not take. After Edgar had gone, the sturdy brain and hand of D. G. Croly took the matter in charge and actually made the growth start. Then the *World*, with him at its head, evoked and published John Fiske's " Lectures on Positivism," far better in their first shape than when pared and cooked over into the " Cosmic Philosophy." Then came the "Modern Thinker" and " Positive Primer." Then Dr. McCosh came out, in reply, with his volume on " Positivism and Christianity." Then Positivist Societies and Liberal Clubs, one after another, were formed and some continue, whence John Elderkin, Henry Evans, James D. Bell, the writer of these lines, and not a few others commenced to ray out the new light, which never has been, and never will

DAVID GOODMAN CROLY.

be extinguished. By the aid of that light let a distant posterity read with gratitude the names of *David G. and Jane Cunningham Croly*, for without them I know it would not have been.

T. B. WAKEMAN.

From a Testimonial by Herbert D. Croly

. . . I should like to relate one incident in the history of my father's relations with myself —an incident which was eminently characteristic of certain aspects of his nature.

From my earliest years it was his endeavor to teach me to understand and believe in the religion of Auguste Comte. One of my first recollections is that of an excursion to Central Park on one bright Sunday afternoon in the spring; there, sitting under the trees, he talked to me on the theme which lay always nearest his heart—that of the solidarity of mankind. There never, indeed, was a time throughout my whole youth, when we were alone together, that he did not return to the same text and impress upon me that a selfish life was no life at all, that " no man liveth for himself, that no man dieth ·for himself." His teachings were as largely negative as positive. While never, perhaps, understanding the Christian religion as a man with a weaker faith in the truth of his own convictions might have understood it, his attitude was one, I judge, of sympathetic scepticism. He was always endeavoring to impress upon me that, while there must necessarily have been something great and good in a faith that had been the inspiration of so many souls, and comfort of mankind through so many centuries, yet at the same time it was incomplete; that very often the followers of Christ gave more to the doctrine than they received from it; and that the teaching of Auguste Comte supplied what was lacking in the teaching of Jesus Christ. His desire to impress upon me a belief which he held himself with all the force of religious conviction led him to attempt explanations which the mind of a child could neither grasp nor retain. He even discussed, for my benefit, theoretical questions as to the existence and nature of the Supreme Being; discussions, of course, that I could so little understand that it was like pouring water on a flat board. It was simply the fulness of his belief that led him to do this. His desire was that, surrounded as I was by people who burnt their candles at the altars of the Christian faith, I should have full opportunity to compare the Positivist *Grand Être* with the Christian Cross. Under such instruction it was not strange that in time I dropped insensibly into his mode of thinking, or, more correctly, into his mode of believing.

While I was at college I was surrounded by other influences, and while retaining everything that was positive and constructive in his teaching,

I dropped the negative cloth in which it was shrouded. My change in opinion was a bitter disappointment to him, as several letters which he wrote at the time testify. But intense as was his disappointment, it never took the form of a reproach. This is very remarkable when we consider what an essential part of his character his beliefs constituted. Here was an end, for which he had striven through many years, failing at the very time when it should have become most fruitful. And his disappointment must have been all the more severe because he exaggerated the differences that existed between us. It was his opinion that his negative opinions were necessarily connected with those which were positive; and that it was impossible truly to hold the one without the other. Yet, as I said, his disappointment never took the form of a reproach. " It is your right; nay, it is even your duty," he used continually to say," to work your own salvation. It has turned out to be different from mine. Well, then, mine is the loss."

From an abstract point of view it may not seem to be so much of a virtue that a father should consider his son's intellectual honesty to be of more importance than his own opinions. But I am not writing from an abstract point of view. We are all but children of the earth; not good, but simply better than the bad. So it was with David G. Croly. His opinions, crystallized by the opposition which they met on every side, were so very much the truth to him that he wished his son to perceive them clearly and cherish them as devoutly as he did.   That wish became impossible of fulfilment.   Part of his life-work had failed. " Mine is the loss."

H. D. CROLY.

From Mr. Croly to His Son Herbert at College

LOTOS CLUB, Oct. 31, 1886.

MY DEAR BOY—You said something about the divergence between my ideas and those of the philosophers whose works you are reading at college.   Let me beg of you to form your own judgment on all the higher themes—religion included —without any reference to what I may have said. All I ask is that you keep your mind open and unpredisposed.   In the language of the Scripture, " prove all things and hold fast to that which is good."   Be careful and do not allow first impressions to influence your maturer judgment.   You say you are reading the controversy between Spencer and Harrison on religion.   In doing so keep in mind the fact that Spencer's matter was revised, while that of Harrison was not; and that upon the latter's protest the work was withdrawn in England.

I wish during your college year that you would read:

(1) Miss Martineau's translation of Comte's "Positive Philosophy."

(2) Mill's Estimate of Comte's Life and Works.

(3) Bridges's Reply to Mill.

(4) All of Frederic Harrison's writings that you can find.

(5) All of Herbert Spencer's works that are not technical.

(6) John Fiske's works.

(7) The works of the English Positivists, such as Congreve, Bridges and Beasley.

By noticing the dates I think you will find that Spencer appropriates a great deal from Comte and that he tries to shirk the obligation. It would be well to read the latter's "General View of Positivism" further along.

My dear son, I shall die happy if I know that you are an earnest student of philosophic themes.

Do cultivate all the religious emotions, reverence, awe, and aspiration, if for no better reason than as a means of self-culture. Educate, train every side of your mental and emotional nature. Read poetry and learn the secret of tears and ecstacy. Go to Catholic and Episcopal churches and surrender yourself to the inspiration of soul-inspiring religious music.

Ever your affectionate

FATHER.

From a Testimonial by Edmund Clarence Stedman

My intimacy with Mr. Croly began in 1860, when we were together upon the editorial staff of the New York *World*. We had many notions, socialistic and otherwise, in common. With these, however, we did not venture to imperil the circulation of that conservative newspaper. He was City Editor, and knew his business. I was struck by the activity of his mind, and his combination of shrewd executive ability with inventive skill. I found him a staunch friend, loyal to his allies, helpful to his subordinates; moreover, a man of strong convictions—which he asserted with a fine dogmatism; an idealist withal, quite unhampered by reverence for conventional usage and opinion. Absolute mental honesty was his chief characteristic.

He was a humanitarian, in the Positivist sense of the word. All his aspirations were for the future glory and happiness of the human race. Faith in the reign of law, and a prophetic certainty of man's elevation—these were his religion. As a thinker and talker he certainly was of the same breed with Tennyson's poet, who

" Sings of what the world will be
When the years have died away."

He bore good fortune and adversity with an equal mind, and he displayed stoical courage throughout prolonged illness of a most depressing type.

Others will add to your own feeling statement of his varied labors. But let me say that, whether our paths came together or diverged, I always thought of him as in every sense a comrade. His loss makes the lessening roll of those with whom I touched elbows in the old newspaper days seem ominously faded.

EDMUND C. STEDMAN.

From a Testimonial by J. D. Bell

Mr. Croly was a great journalist. He was not a great editorial writer, but he was a great editor. He had the true executive temper and power—that is, the ability to obtain from others the work that was in them. He never made the mistake of endeavoring to do everything himself. He was just, as well as generous to his subordinates, and many of the younger journalists have reason to remember his kindness to them. In any company in which he was thrown he was sure to attract attention, and there were very few companies in which he did not take the leading part by virtue of his ability and not of his self-assertion. He never used tobacco in any form, and was otherwise a strictly temperate man. In his utterances he was often very radical, but in practice he was always thoroughly conservative.

His social predilections led him to study the writings of Auguste Comte. He accepted his doctrines and endeavored to popularize them in writings and meetings, but with very limited success. Indeed, he often said that while intellectually Positivism was in the air, as a social doctrine it was too far in advance of the present age to become popular.

He was essentially a family man and loved his home and household. During the greater part of his married life, however, the exacting editorial duties and literary labors of himself and his wife prevented them from enjoying the society of the home circle to the extent that each desired. Here, as in so many other cases, the individual was sacrificed for the benefit of the public.

From a Testimonial by St. Clair McKelway

. . . David G. Croly's personality was always healthy and hopeful. He commended with justice, he censured with consideration, he changed or cut out your copy with regard exclusively to the increased value of the article for newspaper purposes. The staff was like a large family under him. Every one's equal rights were regarded, every one's special talents were stimulated, every one's peculiar fads or foibles were genially borne with. Officially he had no favorites. Personally he chose his friends among the staff as freely as he would do among outsiders. The unrecorded kindnesses of the man were fragrant and not few. To newcomers he would intimate what were the prejudices or susceptibilities or limitations of those among whom they were cast. He would be just as careful to see that the old standbys did not make things rough or unfair for the newcomers. He had little respect for the gifts or views that could not be made interconvertible with newspaper results. He took a public view of party questions and rarely a personal view of any questions. Between what he thought and wished as an iconoclast, a reformer, or a reconstructor of foundations and what he was intrusted to say as an editor, he drew the line sharp and clear. While, as I have remarked, he was rarely a writer with his own hand, the articles which he suggested or poured into or pulled out of others were made so eminently characteristic of himself that they were stamped with his quality as truly as if he had written them himself. He was very proud of the success of the men in after life who started on their newspaper careers under him. He followed them with good wishes always, he spoke strong words for them when, where, and to whom they little suspected, and he rightly regarded their success as a vindication of his own prescience in having set them on their way, and also as a gratification not merely to his confidence in his own opinion concerning them, but to the wishes of his unselfish heart in desiring that they should take the pinnacles of achievement in whatsoever field of newspaper work inclination, necessity, opportunity or destiny marked out before them.

ST. CLAIR MCKELWAY.

The *Eagle* Office, Brooklyn, May 14, 1889.

From a Testimonial by John Elderkin

David G. Croly was a strong man. He was strong in his convictions, his honesty, and his capacity to meet all the requirements of life in the most populous, enterprising, and brilliant city of the continent. His strength begot independence, and he was before all else independent in the formation and expression of his views, both on public affairs and those which are more personal and philosophical. He never apologized for his opinions, and his life needs no apology. His mind dwelt on that side of every question which involved the interest and welfare of the whole mass of mankind, and his religious philosophy was pure Humanitarianism. His reverence for Comte was the result of his intellectual conviction that in his altruistic teaching was to be found the only remedy for the wrongs and sufferings of the world.

In personal intercourse Mr. Croly was suggestive, inspiring and encouraging. It was always with a slight shock to preconceived notions and prejudices that one listened to his comments on any current movement or event, for he was sure to take an original and characteristic view which could not be calculated.

From Mrs. Croly's Contribution to Her Husband's Memorial

Mr. Croly was in his twenty-seventh year when I first knew him, but as yet had made no mark in journalism. He had not found his place in it. He was employed as City Editor of the New York *Herald*—a position which had not then developed the importance which attaches to it to-day—and his duties consisted mainly of making out the " slate " for the staff of reporters, and doing such reportorial work as it was the province and habit of the City Editor to perform. This afforded little scope for a man of Mr. Croly's latent power; and his dissatisfaction and desire to find a new field was the cause of our going West within three years after our marriage and starting a daily paper in a Western town. Had the town been larger the story would have been different. As it was, we spent our money, not without result; for Mr. Croly discovered that his forte was not execution, but direction, and that his fertility of brain only needed a sufficiently wide field to develop powers capable of greater expansion.

He was the most utterly destitute of the mechanical or "doing" faculty of any man I ever saw, and never used his own hands if he could possibly help it. But ideas flowed freely upon all subjects in which he was interested, and he distributed them as freely, knowing that the reservoir though forever emptied was always full. This amazing fertility was in some respects a detriment, for it led him into too many projects, and made him careless whom he enriched, while his dislike of the mechanism of his work made profit for others at his expense. I know no other journalist in New York City, during my own journalistic career of thirty-three years, who has made so many and such diverse publications, or put so much originality and force into the detail of his work. The *World*, and particularly the Sunday *World*, which was the foundation of the Sunday newspaper, the New York illustrated *Graphic*, the *Round Table*, and other journals were built up by his energy, and owed their most striking and successful features to his suggestiveness. He was particularly unselfish in his estimate of other men and his appreciation of their work. He was as proud of discovering the good qualities of a man on his staff as a miner of finding a nugget, and never wearied of expatiating upon them. Indeed, he did this more than once to his own disadvantage, thus furnishing an instrument to treachery. I am sure the "boys" of the old *World* staff,

St. Clair McKelway, A. C. Wheeler (" Nym Crinkle"), T. E. Wilson, H. G. Crickmore, Montgomery Schuyler, E. C. Stedman, and others, will look back with a little sigh for the " old times," and for the generous recognition they received from one who was never at a loss for a subject, or for the treatment of a topic, and was always a good comrade and heart and soul sympathizer in their work, its trials and its achievements.

A chief quality with Mr. Croly was faithfulness to the interests he served. This was put to some severe tests; but they could not be called temptations, for disloyalty did not present itself as a possibility to him. His faults were those of a nervous temperament, combined with great intellectual force and a strength of feeling which in some directions and under certain circumstances became prejudice. He could never, in any case, be made to run a machine. He hated the obvious way of saying or doing a thing. He cultivated the " unexpected" almost to a fault, and always gave a touch of originality even to the commonplace. His pessimistic and unhopeful temperament was doubtless due to inherent and hereditary bodily weakness, and to the lack of muscular cultivation in his youth, which might have modified inherent tendencies. His mental lack was form not force; and he had enough original elemental ideas to have supplied a dozen men. In that respect he was superior to every other journalist I have ever known—not excepting Horace Greeley, Henry J. Raymond and Frederick Hudson.

But the time has gone by for ideas. It is not that they are a drug in the market, but that there is no market for them. To-day is the apotheosis of the commonplace, the iteration of the cries of the street, the gabble of the sidewalk, and the gossip of the tea-table; neither originality nor force is needed for such journalism as this, and they may therefore well rest to the music of the pines.

One of the strongest influences in Mr. Croly's life was his acquaintance with the Positivist movement in England, and his interest in the works of Auguste Comte. Up to this time he had experienced none of the undoubted benefit which accrues to every man and woman from the possession of an ideal standard, and settled convictions which inspire or take the place of religious aspiration. Positivism did all this for Mr. Croly, so far as anything could, and he became one of its most eager and devoted adherents.

Mr. T. B. Wakeman, himself one of the earliest and most able leaders, credits Mr. Croly with being the "father" of the movement in this country, and in fact he was the first to make known that any representative of Positivist ideas existed in America. He invited and paid for the first lecture ever delivered in New York City upon the subject; it was given by Mr. Edgar, an unknown

" apostle," in a little hall (De Garmo) on the
corner of 14th street and Fifth avenue, on a
certain Sunday some twenty or more years ago.
The result of the lecture was that a dozen people
formed a little society and engaged Mr. Edgar to
give them a series of Sunday talks on the practical
bearings of the religion of humanity.   Mr. Edgar
was not in himself an interesting exponent of his
ideas, but his message inculcated duty, love to
man, a life open and free from concealments, the
possession of personal gifts or acquired property
as trusts to be used for the good of others, and the
recognition of value in all that has been and is.

These ideas became more or less an actuating
principle.   They brought together a circle of men
and women of the best quality, who endeavored
to live up to their standard, and by work and
daily life, rather than by active propagandism, to
crystallize opinions into a vital force.   For several
years the regular meetings were held at our house,
the " festivals " of the year being often given at
the residences of other members of the society—
Mr. T. B Wakeman, or Mr. Courtlandt Palmer.
There is still an " old guard " left, of as good,
brave, and unselfish men and women as ever
walked on this earth, and though some differed
from Mr. Croly, and from each other on some
points, yet they all knew and acknowledged that
he brought to them the beginning of the best inspiration of their lives.

Mr. Croly's latest expressed wish was that all the usual forms should be disregarded in the event of his death, except the simplest service and the presence of flowers. " If any one thinks enough of me," he said, " to bring me flowers, let them; but have no elaborate mourning, and bury me close to the earth, near the pines, and facing the sea. The legend he left for his grave-stone was: " I meant well, tried a little, failed much." But this will not be the verdict of those who came under the influence of his strong and many-sided personality.

Mrs. Croly's Club Life

Mrs. Croly's Club Life

By Haryot Holt Dey

THERE is a pleasant and not irrational fancy in the mind of the writer that somewhere in space there exists the abiding-place of ideas, and that as fast as earth-dwellers are ready for them they are released. Like a bird the idea takes flight and seeks a home in the brain of some one who is singled out to forward and exploit it for the benefit of humanity. Thenceforward, that person becomes the apostle of the idea. " We are not in the possession of our ideas," says Heine, " but are possessed by them; they master us and force us into the arena where like gladiators we must fight for them." But it is only to the elect that great ideas are assigned, one who either through heredity or by special development is qualified to carry the message. This fanciful reasoning applies admirably to the idea for women's clubs— organizations for women—and in its selection of Jenny June it made no mistake in the character of its agent.

The first woman's club was organized in March, 1868, and was the outcome of feminine protest,

because women were barred from the reception
and banquet tendered to Charles Dickens by the
Press Club of New York City.   Among those
who applied for tickets on equal grounds with
men was Mrs. Croly, then an active, recognized
force in journalism, and when the idea of a woman's club took possession of her she had become
the most indignant and spirited woman ever
locked out of a banquet hall.

Forty years ago it required courage for a woman
to step aside from the ranks of conservatism and
organize a woman's club; it was regarded as a
side issue of " woman's rights," a movement then
in grave disrepute.   But Mrs. Croly had dared
untrodden paths once before when she stepped
into the field of journalism, and her experience
there had developed self-confidence.   She had
been writing for women for many years, and
through her mission had acquired instinctive
knowledge of their needs; and so when the affront
was put upon her by her male colleagues of the
press she conceived the idea of a club for women.
It should be one that would manage its own
affairs, represent as far as possible the active interests of women, and create a bond of fellowship
between them, which many women as well as
men thought at that time would be impossible of
accomplishment.   Mrs. Croly wrote in her "History of Clubs" thirty years later: "At this period
no one of those connected with the undertaking

had ever heard of a woman's club, or of any secular organization composed entirely of women for the purpose of bringing all kinds of women together to work out their objects in their own way." And then again: " When the history of the nineteenth century comes to be written women will appear as organizers and leaders of great organized movements among their own sex for the first time in the history of the world."

" The originator specially disavowed any specific object, only asking for a representative woman's organization based on perfectly equal terms in which women might acquire methods, learn how to work together for general objects, not for charity or a propaganda."

" This declaration of principles was the cause of much abusive criticism, as well as failure to obtain aid and sympathy. Had Sorosis started to *do* any one thing, from building an asylum for aged and indigent 'females' to supplying the natives of Timbuctoo with pocket handkerchiefs, it would have found a public already made. But its attitude was frankly ignorant and inquiring. It laid no claims to wisdom or knowledge that could be of any use to anybody. It simply felt the stirring of an intense desire that women should come together—all together, not from one church, or one neighborhood, or one walk of life, but from all quarters, and take counsel together, find the cause of separations and failures, of ignorance and

6

wrong-doing, and try to discover better ways, more intelligent methods."

Under this banner Sorosis was launched. Alice Cary was its first president. The story of Sorosis from the beginning is a very interesting one; from the view-point of the press its doings and sayings and business affairs generally have always afforded subject-matter for comment and conjecture. Of its early days Mrs. Croly wrote: "The social events of the first year were memorable, for they were the first of their kind, and practically changed the custom of confining public dinner-giving to men. The first was offered as an *amende honorable* on the part of the New York Press Club, and consisted of a 'breakfast' to which the Press Club invited Sorosis, but did not invite it to speak or do anything but sit still and eat, and be talked and sung to. The second was a 'tea' given by Sorosis to the Press Club at which it reversed the order, furnishing all the speakers and allowing the men no chance, not even to respond to their own toast. The third was a 'dinner,'—the brightest and best of the whole—at which the ladies and gentlemen each paid their own way and shared equally the honors and responsibilities." This is said to be the first public dinner at which men and women ever sat down on equal terms. A report of it in a daily newspaper closed as follows: "The entire affair was one of the most delightful events of the season, and will long be held in pleasantest memory by all who had the honor to participate in it. We believe we violate no secret when we say that the gentlemen were most agreeably surprised to find their rival club composed of charming women, representing the best aristocracy of the metropolis, an aristocracy of sterling good sense, earnest thought, aspiration and progressive intellect, with no perceptible taint of strong-mindedness."

The growth and expansion of Sorosis were watched by Mrs. Croly with the same eager interest with which a mother contemplates the development of a child, not knowing just how its character will shape, guarding it always with love, for a potential force in its directing. It was her spirit that steered it over rough places; that brought harmony out of discord; that inspired, soothed, provided wise counsel, and that many times sacrificed personal feelings for the good of the whole. To do this required mental qualities of a high order—courage, foresight, judgment, and not a little of the martyr spirit. Women had never organized before, and the conditions to be met and the problems to be solved stood absolutely alone, with no precedent to build upon or decide even the simplest question. What firmness was required in the leader at that time, when, for example, women who had been her staunchest allies deserted the ranks because they could not select the club name! It was a firm hand that kept

the unorganized body from going to pieces on the
rocks of dissension, and it was at that time that the
leader proved her inalienable right to her title.
She had led women into the field of journalism,
and now she was leading them into organization.
Clubs began to form in all parts of the country,
and when Sorosis arrived at its twenty-first birthday, it was Mrs. Croly's idea that they should all
come together, and when the invitation was issued
they came.   Thus was formed the General Fed-
cration of Women's Clubs.   At present there are
800,000 women belonging to that federation; each
State has its own federation, New York forming
first, at Mrs. Croly's suggestion, and now containing 32,000 enrolled members.   The General
Federation was formed in 1889.   The writer recalls the triumph in Mrs. Croly's tone when she
replied to the appeal of a man who came to her to
beg to be given the names of the women belonging to the federation.   " If you choose to send a
woman to copy the names," she said, " you may
do so, but it will take her more than a week."
And the General Federation was less than three
years old at the time.

Mrs. Croly organized the Woman's Press Club
of New York in 1889.   It is due to her wisdom
that it was carried through many crises.   She
was its president from the day it was founded to
the day of her death; always its loving teacher,
her enthusiasm regarding its development never

flagged. She lived to see it firmly established, a harmonious and delightful organization, and she was satisfied.

Mrs. Croly was neither parliamentarian, orator, nor politician, but she had a fund of good sense, wise judgment, and a power of expression which could clarify an atmosphere when mere knowledge of the " Rules of Order " would have failed. She had spiritual vision, and by it she knew the soul of the club; no amount of dissension could shake her faith in its ultimate good, and in times of crisis she presided with a serenity only accountable in the fact that she viewed from the mountain summit what her associates saw only from the housetop. What years of development she enjoyed long before the club idea possessed her, endowing her with wisdom and mental breadth, and what associations that urged and demanded that she become a student of sociology! The seeds of thought planted in those early days of journalistic experience, inclusive of what she terms the " Positivist Episode," blossomed in her later, more mature years, and all the harvest she brought and applied to the organization of women. To the casual observer an organized body of women differed in no particular form from any ordinary assembly of women. What it was to her one can only realize by a careful perusal of her writings on club formation, and the moral awakening that sounded the bugle note of progress when women began to organize.

Once it came to the hearing of this gentle apostle
of development, that she had been said to represent a cult.   The occasion was a reception given
in her honor by one of her clubs on her seventieth
birthday.   There had been speeches and congratulations, and the scene was one of general rejoicing.
" Oh, she is the leader of a cult," whispered a
guest, and the remark was repeated to Mrs. Croly.
She received it with a sorry smile of regret that
any one should so misinterpret the significance of
the scene.   As if the narrow and exclusive word
"cult" could be applied to an assembly that stood
for organization and human development, which,
in her prophetic vision, only needed time to unite
races, and ultimately to extend around the globe.
To her it signified " the opening of the door, the
stepping out into the freedom of the outer air,
and the sweet sense of fellowship with the whole
universe, that comes with liberty and light."
Few women carry their enthusiasm till past
three-score-and-ten, as Mrs. Croly did.   With the
failing of physical strength the wand of power
passed into the hands of younger women whom
she hailed as her successors, and whose growth
and development were the blossoms springing
from the seed she herself had planted; and in the
last years of her noble life, when the glow of sun-
set was on the garden of her activities, the love
she bore her fellow-women was her unfailing joy
and inspiration.

At the time of life when people recognize the fact that their forces are waning, and that a well-earned period of rest has arrived, Mrs. Croly set for herself the last task of her busy life. She felt she had something to tell about the success of her great idea, her message to women, and she wrote the " History of the Woman's Club Movement in America," a volume containing eleven hundred and eighty pages, which told the story of nearly all the clubs in the General Federation. This book will remain a monument to the founder of women's clubs. Into it she put the skill and experience of her long years of editorship, urging every faculty to the work, and applying herself with a degree of industry that characterized the zeal of her best working years. And it testifies to the martyr-like nature of her spirit, that she even rallied from the disappointment consequent upon the financial failure of the book. The dedication of the work reads as follows: " This book has been a labor of love, and it is lovingly dedicated to the Twentieth Century Woman by one who has seen and shared in the struggles of the Woman of the Nineteenth Century." But nothing that is good is lost, and the book testifies to the illimitable ideas, the trust in eternal goodness, and the strength of purpose of one who had a glorified estimate of latent feminine forces that require to be developed.

Essays and Addresses by Jane Cunningham Croly

Beginnings of Organization[1]

Women in Religious Organization

WHEN the history of the Nineteenth Century comes to be written, women will appear for the first time in the history of the world as organizers, and leaders of great organized movements among their own sex.

The world of to-day, both for men and women, is a different world from that which furnished the outlook for the men and women of a hundred years ago. Science, invention, have changed its material aspects; and while retiring some individual activities and occupations, they have created new fields of industry that are rapidly changing the face of the world, and making new demands upon strength and energy.

The world which man has conquered, and is still conquering, is no longer the purely physical. He is working now toward the discovery and control of the powers of the air, and has already harnessed some of them to do his bidding. The succession of great events and discoveries will mark this century as an epoch in the world's

[1] *History of the Woman's Club Movement in America.*

history, and is responsible for economic changes which create social disturbance, and to which both men and women must adjust themselves, often without knowing the why or wherefore of that which is so different from what has been. It is one of the paradoxes in human nature that women, while being made responsible for human conditions, have been condemned to individual isolation.   It has been largely the result of general physical differentiation and the dependence that grew out of it, and, secondarily, the long ages required to produce settled social conditions and a reversal of that great unwritten law of kings and men—that might made right.

It is true that there was a time, some traditions of which are still preserved among the Indian tribes of North America, when the woman possessed controlling influence and power.   This matriarchal or mother age passed with the primitive period in which the energies of men were absorbed in hunting and fighting.   It was a tribal effort through tribal women to formulate and give importance to family life, and it must have been accepted and more or less sanctioned by the men. This tribal leadership, at first domestic and social, disappeared with the development of military leaders, the acquisition of military powers, and the centralization of property in lands, houses, and personal belongings, that required constant and effective methods of protection and defence.

Instances are not wanting of heroic women of those early days who were capable of holding and defending person and property against aggression and warfare. But the logic of events was strong then, as now, and the destiny of the woman was not that of military supremacy.

The first step in associated life taken by women was a simple protest against the use and abuse of power on the part of men, wrought up by fear or loathing to the point of desperation. Women, usually of rank, fled to the desert with one or two companions, and encountered unheard-of hardships rather than submit to the fate to which they had been condemned by father, brother, or some other man who could exercise authority over them. The first Church-sisterhood grew out of such beginnings, and gradually obtained the sanction of the Church. A recent remarkable work, ''Women in Monasticism,'' shows how wide and powerful the system of religious sisterhoods had become as early as the fifth century, and traces its growing strength and enlargement until its decline, which was coeval with the Reformation.

The strength of this extraordinary development lay in the fact that it furnished women with a vocation; it gave employment to faculty. The sisterhoods of the convents and monasteries were the nurses, the teachers, the students, the caretakers of the poor, and the guardians of the

orphaned rich.   The Fathers of the Church—St.
Jerome, St. Chrysostom, St. Augustine—all bear
witness to the high character of these sisterhoods
and to their individual members, to their virtues
and lives of self-sacrificing devotion.   Many of
these women became learned by the exercise of
memory alone, for they had no books.   Many
enriched their convents with manuscript books—
the result of lives of painstaking labor.   The
Beguines, who founded hospitals and schools,
were the best educated women of their day—the
eleventh century.   They read Tacitus and Virgil
in the original, and were skilled in medicine.
Disease often took loathsome forms, and only women whose lives were consecrated to self-denying
labor could have been the patient ministers to the
diseased poor.

This is all the more noteworthy because the
idea of vocation was not the early incentive to
monastic life.   It was sought as a refuge; it developed into a vocation; and it is a matter of interest to women to-day that these spontaneous
vocations, growing out of an enforced life, were
inspired by love of well-doing, desire for study, the
acquisition of knowledge, its distribution, and the
ever-ready spirit of helpfulness at the sacrifice of
every personal indulgence.

Naturally the monastic life of women was controlled by the Church, and could have continued
to exist only by permission.   A Spanish lady of

rank who had befriended Ignatius Loyola as a young student of Barcelona, attracted by the odor of sanctity and scholarship which attached itself to the Order which he founded, gained reluctant permission to establish (1545) an Order of Jesuitesses, subject to the same strict rules and discipline. This was the beginning of a strictly woman's Jesuit "college," which flourished notwithstanding all the efforts Loyola himself made to get rid of it, and the restrictions put upon it. Many noble ladies joined it, and it became the foundation of a number of houses of the same name and character, extending into Flanders and England, when, without cause, except fear perhaps of their extent and influence, they were finally suppressed by a bull of Pope Urban VIII, bearing date, January 13, 1630. This Order of Jesuitesses existed for nearly a century. Their colleges were scholastic, and had given rise to preparatory schools, when they were summarily suppressed because of their independent life.

Had this Order continued to exist it might have gained an educational ascendency throughout Europe which even the strong wave of the Reformation would have found it hard to overcome. But the convents and monasteries generally suffered at this time from the abuses which had crept into the Church, and the rage for power which possessed its prelates.

The influence was mischievous also from a

social and domestic point of view; from the
sanctity and superiority attached to those who
ignored natural ties and duties, thus lowering
the social and domestic standard, and setting the
nun's habit above the woman, the wife and the
mother. Yet nature had asserted itself even in
the convent. The motherhood in the monastic
woman made her the mother, the caretaker, the
nurse, the teacher, and the helper of all those
who needed maternal care, while condemning and
ignoring its common aspects and place in every-
day life.

This absence of domestic ties was not, however,
obligatory upon all sisterhoods. An interesting
story of the " First Council of Women," told by
Madame Lentier at the Congress of Women in
Paris in 1889, bears upon this point.

The monastic school out of which the Council
grew, was founded in the early part of the seventh
century, by Iduberge, wife of Pepin, mayor under
the Frankish kings.

Iduberge cleared a space in the forest, and built
a house for the education and religious consecra-
tion (if they desired it) of the daughters of nobles,
her daughter Gertrude becoming the abbess. No
vow of celibacy was imposed. As long as they
remained in the abbey they were to conform to
the rules of the house, but if they desired to
marry they were free to leave. The *chanoinesses*
of Nivelle spent their morning in religious duties,

but the rest of the day they were at liberty to mix with the outer world. The abbess alone took upon herself the vow of perpetual virginity. A hundred and seventy passed away after the death of Gertrude. The abbey had grown in power, had gathered around itself a town with gates and towers and fortifications, but was independent of the French Government, being under the sole rule of the abbess, who was called the "Princess."

This independence excited the jealousy of the Church, and in May, 820, Nivelle received a visit from Valcand, the reigning bishop of Liège. He was received by the lady abbess in the habit of her order, a cross of gold in her hand; mounted on a white horse she rode at the head of the procession that marched to meet him. Young girls of noble birth, clad in long white gowns trimmed with ermine, and mounted on palfreys, followed their abbess, and behind them the town authorities, feudal lords and administrators of justice.

At the same time Valcand entered the town with every honor and courtesy due to his rank. He held a solemn service, and having given the benediction, he rose again and addressed the *chanoinesses*. He declared that it had been decided by the Council of Aix-la-Chapelle that he should be sent to Nivelle to enforce the rules of St. Benoit, which must be followed by all religious bodies; this rule being that all the devotees of Nivelle were required to take upon themselves the

vow of perpetual virginity, to acknowledge themselves dependent upon their bishop in all secular
matters, and finally to yield up to Valcand all
temporal power at Nivelle.

This solemn declaration was received in silence.
For some moments no one moved or spoke, but
a low murmur swept over the young sisters of
Nivelle Abbey.   The lady abbess, followed by
her *chanoinesses*, rose and advanced to the rails
of the choir stand. ' The abbess Hiltrude, daughter of Lyderic II, sovereign of Flanders under the
emperor, then between thirty-five and forty years
of age, was beautiful; of that calm, grave type
which speaks of a quiet, well-regulated life.

" In the name of the Cloister of St. Gertrude,"
she said, " we protest against any interference in
the temporal power of this government.   We
claim the right of taking to ourselves husbands
when it seems right to us so to do.   We are
therefore resolved to follow the rules of our patron
saint, as we always have done heretofore, and if
this protest is insufficient we will present our appeal to our Holy Father, the Pope."

The bishop declared that he would maintain the
rule given by the Council at Aix, and then descending from the pulpit, he ordered his people to
follow him at once out of Nivelle, refusing to join
in any of the festivities prepared in his honor.

Hiltrude now took things seriously into her
own hands, leaving nothing undone to secure the

success of her appeal. She sent a courier to the Pope, and another to Louis le Debonaire; but the wise abbess took yet further precautions: she at once organized a council at Nivelle of all the abbesses of the French Empire, requiring silence from them, and assuring them of security in the town. The council could not be brought together for a year, but on the 1st of May, 821, Hiltrude inaugurated her " Concile de Femmes."

She took advantage of the marriage of Count d'Albion with Regina, which was to take place at the abbey. Regina was a *chanoinesse*, and it was the custom when a member of the circle at the abbey married, that the marriage should be solemnized at Nivelle. Fifteen titled abbesses, all of aristocratic lineage, arrived with imposing suites. The council was a short one. They approved of all that Hiltrude had done, and signed the appeal. The document, written, signed, and sealed by all the abbesses present, was immediately sent to Rome, and to Valcand himself. Meantime the pope and the king, who were much perplexed, and the bishop, who was completely baffled by the logic, strength and force of appeal of the " Concile," were obliged to withdraw the oppositiou, and the *chanoinesses* were left in peace to marry or not to marry, as they pleased.

The ancient order of deaconesses imposed no vow, yet it was co-existent with the early church, and accepted by many of the fathers as part of the apostolic order.   This position was strengthened by the high character of the women, many of them widows, or unprotected women, whom death or some other calamity had freed from natural ties.

Ancient church history is full of the records of courage, devotion, and self-sacrifice on the part of these women, who were generally of high birth, but gave themselves to poverty and the most menial offices, and left names which have perpetuated the sanctity of their order, and come down to the present day as types of good women.

The ceremonies used in the ordination of a deaconess were precisely the same as those used for a deacon.   The deaconesses were not cloistered: they lived at home with children or relatives.   But they wore a distinctive dress, and had their place in the church with the clergy.   The "golden age" of the order is said to have been immediately following the apostolic era, before the spirit of monasticism had destroyed or limited activities, and shut off sympathy with the outside world.

The royal and imperial order of the Hadraschin in Prague, Germany, is the most imposing relic remaining of the religious orders of women, though not the most numerous.   There are about forty chapters still in existence of this ancient order, with a royal residence at Prague.   The abbess possessed the right to crown the queen at coronation ceremonies, and exercised it as late as

1836, wearing all the magnificent insignia of her rank in the order.

A more numerous order of consecrated women, presided over and governed by one "mother-general," is that of St. Joseph de Cluny. This was founded by a woman, Madame Javonbey, in the beginning of the present century, about ninety years ago. It has one hundred and twenty-eight houses in France, and two in the United States. It has others in South America, one in Italy, several in the West Indies and some in Africa.

All its property is in community, and its membership—about six thousand women—teach in its schools, and care for the sick poor in hospitals and in their homes. Two hundred are assigned to the care of the insane, by the French Government.

The mother-general administers, from the mother-house (*maison mère*) at Paris. She has two assistants and a council of six sisters. Under the mother-general there are mother-superiors, one to each estate, administering and governing it, but under this mother-superior at Paris. These lesser governing women send in weekly reports to the home convent at Paris, giving brief accounts of transactions and events, such as the entrance of pupils, the purchase of lands, and extra dole of food to the poor, the death of a member and the like. They are a prosperous, working sisterhood, and have preserved the integrity and independence of their beginning.

It was the spirit of protest against church and monastic abuses, embodied in Martin Luther, which broke up the monastic system for both men and women. Doubtless also it had outlived its usefulness in any large or general sense. A more settled social and domestic life was becoming possible through the development of trades and industries, while the domestic virtues in women began to acquire a value, and furnish guarantees to the State.

The discovery of printing gave a tremendous impulse to the spread of civilizing and educational influences, to the multiplication of schools, and the desire for knowledge. It was the dawn of intellectual freedom, and the school of the people was the open door for it.

Spiritual freedom had to wait longer. It waited the unfolding of the woman. At the beginning of this century she was still under the dominion of the church and its leaders, and her efforts were controlled by sects and doctrines.

The first associated work of women in this country, and in this century, was still religious and philanthropic. The " Sisters of Charity " in America owes its origin to a young and beautiful New York woman, Elizabeth Seton, who was born in 1774, married at twenty, but lost her husband by death in a very few years. Obliged to support herself, she opened a school in Baltimore. But her tendency was toward the devoted life of a *religieuse*, and the gift of a foundation fund enabled her to gratify this strong desire. She assumed the conventual habit, and opened a convent school on July 30, 1809, in Emmetsburg, of which she became mother-superior. The character of "Mother" Seton was considered saintly by Protestants and Roman Catholics alike. She died at her post in 1821, after a life the last half of which was entirely spent in self-denying work. Mrs. Seton was exceedingly lovely as a young woman; and her sweet, serene face and presence, as she grew older, was said to exert a magical influence upon all who came in contact with her. This was particularly seen in her care of the sick, and in dealing with turbulent spirits: they came immediately under her influence without any effort on her part.

The first ten years of the present century saw the beginning of a number of religious societies of women, organized to create funds, and aid in church mission work. First among these were the "cent" societies, 1801 and 1804, and later the Woman's Auxiliaries to the Board of Foreign Missions. These grew in size and strength, until in 1839 there were six hundred and eighty-eight of these societies. But, unfortunately, their limited and purely subjective character afforded small basis for the wider growth necessary to perpetuity, and they gradually declined, until in 1860 they had become nearly extinct.

A little later, 1864, the first independent "Union" of women missionary workers was formed in New York by Mrs. Doremus, and within a few years every denomination, beginning with the Congregationalists, had its organized Woman's Auxiliary to the American Board of Home and Foreign Missions. The "Missionary Union" remains, however, the only independent society of women workers in this field, managing its own affairs, raising its own funds, and sending out its own missionaries, both men and women. Its very existence has been a great strength to the Woman's Auxiliaries, stimulating them to independent action, and especially to the demand for a voice in the disposal of the large sums they raise and turn over to the treasury of the American Board.

The oldest purely women-societies in this country were also started for missionary and church work. The first is the "Female Charitable Society" of Baldwinsville, N. J., and is still existent.

The object of the Baldwinsville society, as stated in the constitution, was "to obtain a more perfect view on the infinite excellence of the Christian religion in its own nature, the importance of making this religion the chief concern of our hearts, the necessity of promoting it in our families, and of diffusing it among our fellow sinners." A further object is "to afford aid to religious institutions, and for the carrying out of this purpose a contribution of twelve and a half cents is required at every quarterly meeting.''

Mrs. Jane Hamill presided at its first meeting; the Rev. John Davenport opened it with prayer. Mrs. Hamill was still the presiding officer at its jubilee anniversary in 1867. At its seventy-eighth annual meeting Mrs. Payn Bigelow was elected president.

The ''Piqua (Ohio) Female Bible Society'' was founded in 1818. It consisted at first of nine women. In those early days the country was a wilderness. Other members were added later. It has had in all, over nine hundred members. Mrs. Elizabeth Pettit was its presiding officer from 1840 until 1881—forty-one years. The daughters and the granddaughters are all made members by right of inheritance, and in several instances four generations have been represented at one time. It held its seventy-fifth anniversary in 1893, when all the descendants of the early members were notified, and many were present. It has held a meeting on the first Monday afternoon of each month for seventy-eight years, and the records are preserved intact. The founder was Mrs. Rachael Johnston, wife of the Indian agent. It has sent over fifteen thousand dollars to the parent Bible Society in New York.

It should be remembered that down to the last quarter of the present century, there was little sympathy with organizations of women, not expressly religious, charitable, or intended to promote charitable objects. "What is the object?" was the first question asked of any organization of women, and if it was not the making of garments, or the collection of funds for a church or philanthropic purpose, it was considered unworthy of attention, or injurious doubts were thrown upon its motives. In Germany, even yet, societies of women are not permitted, except such as have a distinctly religious, educational or charitable object.

The Moral Awakening[1]

THE life of the world is continuous, morally and spiritually as well as materially. The individual sees it at short range and in fragments. That is the reason why it so often seems dislocated and out of joint. A thoughtful writer, Mrs. L. R. Zerbe, says: " When Goethe made his discovery of the unity of structure in organic life, he gave to the philosophers, who had long taught the value, the ' sovereignty ' of the individual, a physiological argument against oppression and tyranny, and put the whole creation on an equal footing."

The dignity of mind, and the right of the individual to its conscious use and possession, had been already clearly enunciated by Fichte, Herder, and others, who antedated Goethe. But Goethe went farther. He carried the discovery of the rights of the individual to its logical conclusion, which was, that the rights of every created thing should be given a hearing. This was absolutely new doctrine. It brought women and children within the pale of humanity. It moralized and humanized nature itself; bringing birds, trees,

[1] *History of the Woman's Club Movement in America.*

flowers, all animate life, into the " brotherhood " of creation.

The writings of Rousseau and Châteaubriand extended the idea, and Madame de Staël and Mary Wollstonecraft were the natural outgrowths of it. It may be said indeed to have been the actuating principle of modern literature, especially of modern English poetry, which vitalizes and idealizes children and nature. Whatever credit may be given to others, it should never be forgotten that to Goethe we owe the discovery of structural unity, that the cell of all organic life is the same.

The ideas that grew out of this discovery reached the higher, thinking class, and inspired the poets with a new enthusiasm for humanity long before it reached the masses. The French nobility were satiated with power. The " Little Trianon " was the only reaction possible to a queen, from the wearisome magnificence of Versailles, the gilded slavery of the court. The people recognized no sentiment of human sympathy in the so-called " whims " and " caprices " of the luxurious occupants of palaces; and maddened by countless wrongs, precipitated the French Revolution, which, it has been said, turned back the tide of progress for one hundred years.

From this movement were developed all those reforms which have made the nineteenth century glorious, monumental in the history of progressive civilization. The abolition of slavery, the development of a spirit of mercy towards dumb animals, the recognition of the human rights of women and children—all these may be traced through many a winding way, back to the German scientists and philosophers, who rediscovered the inner life while working from its outer side.

Yet, as in history there are no sporadic instances, no isolated facts, so this flower of our century—the recognition of the rights of all created things, with all that it involves — belongs to universal history. It is the product of the Reformation and the Renaissance, with roots only the records of Rome and Greece and Egypt may discover.

The quickening of moral and spiritual life in our day, its accelerated movement, is not to be claimed by or traced to any one set of influences or propaganda. The awakening has been all along the line; and it has resulted in a new mental attitude toward the human life of the world, both as a whole and in its various parts. Its great outcome is the learning to live with, rather than for, others.

This new view, this great advance of the moral and spiritual forces, addressed itself with singular significance to women. To those who were prepared, it came not only as an awakening, but as emancipation—emancipation of the soul, freedom from the tyranny of tradition and prejudice, and the acquisition of an intellectual outlook; a spiritual liberty achieved so quietly as to be unnoticed except by those who watched the progress of this bloodless revolution, and the falling away of the shackles that bind the spirit in its early and often painful effort to reach the light.

The broadening of human sympathy, the freedom of will, gave rise to a thousand new forms of activity; some of these an expansion of those which had previously existed; others opening new channels of communication; all looking towards wider fields of effort, a larger unity, a more complete realization of the eternal ideal, the fatherhood of God, the motherhood of woman, the brotherhood of man.

Realization of this ideal brought a new conception of duty to the mind of woman, unlocked the strong gates of theological and social tradition, and opened the windows of her soul to a new and more glorious world. The sense of duty is always strong in the woman. If she disregards it she never ceases to suffer. Her convictions of it have made her the most willing and joyful of martyrs, the most persistent and relentless of bigots, the most blind and devoted of partisans, the most faithful and believing of friends, and the only type out of which Nature could form the mother. This quality has made women the constructive force they are in the world, and gives all the more importance to the new departure, to the influences of the new sources of enlargement that have come into their lives.

Thus it became a necessity that the quickening of conscience, the widening of sympathy, the influence of aggregations, the stimulus to desire and ambitions, should be accompanied by corresponding growth in knowledge and a love beyond the narrow confines of family and church.

The cry of the woman emerging from a darkened past was " light, more light," and light was breaking. Gradually came the demand and the opportunity for education; for intellectual freedom for women as well as men; for cultivation of gifts and faculties. The early half of the century was marked by a crusade for the cause of the better education of women, as significant as that for the physical emancipation of the slave, and as devoted on the part of its leaders.

Simultaneous with this were two other movements — the anti-slavery agitation, inspired by the new enthusiasm for human rights and carried on largely by the Quakers of both sexes. The woman's-rights movement was the natural outgrowth of the individual-sovereignty idea which the German philosophers had planted, and of which Mary Wollstonecraft was the first great woman-exponent.

The keynote of the educational advance was struck by Emma Willard in 1821. She was followed by Mary Lyon, Mary Mortimer, and other brave women who dared to ask for women the cultivation of such faculties as they possessed, without let or hindrance. This demand has taken the century to develop and enforce. The work was so gradual that it is not yet, by any means, accomplished. Schools and colleges exist, but not yet equally, except here and there. They are, however, giving us an army of trained women who are bringing the force of knowledge to bear upon questions which have heretofore only enlisted sympathies.

Simultaneously with this question of educational opportunity, has arisen an eager seeking after knowledge on the part of women who have been debarred from its enjoyment, or lacked opportunity for its acquisition. The knowledge sought was not that of a limited, sectional geography, or a mathematical quantity as taught in schools, but the knowledge of the history and development of races and peoples, of the laws and principles that underlie this development, and the place of the woman in this grand march of the ages.

The woman has been the one isolated fact in the universe. The outlook upon the world, the means of education, the opportunities for advancement, had all been denied her; and that "community of feeling and sense of distributive justice which grows out of coöperative interests in work and life, had found small opportunity for growth or activity."

The opportunity came with the awakening of the communal spirit, the recognition of the law of the solidarity of interests, the sociological advance which established a basis of equality among a wide diversity of conditions and individuals, and opportunities for all capable of using them. This great advance was not confined to a society or a neighborhood; it did not require subscription to a tenet, or the giving up of one's mode of life. It was simply a change of a point of view, the opening of a door, the stepping out into the freedom of the outer air, and the sweet sense of fellowship with the whole universe that comes with liberty and light.

The difference was only a point of view, but it changed the aspect of the world. This new note, which meant for the woman liberty, breadth and unity, was struck by the woman's club.

To the term " club," as applied to and by women, may be fitly referred the words in which John Addington Symonds defines Renaissance. " This," he remarks, " is not explained by this or that characteristic, but as an effort for which at length the time has come." It means the attainment of the conscious freedom of the woman spirit, and has been manifested first most strongly and most widely in this country, because here that spirit has attained the largest measure of freedom.

The woman's club was not an echo; it was not the mere banding together for a social and economic purpose, like the clubs of men. It became at once, without deliberate intention or concerted action, a light-giving and seed-sowing centre of purely altruistic and democratic activity. It had no leaders. It brought together qualities rather than personages; and by a representation of all interests, moral, intellectual, and social, a natural and equal division of work and opportunity, created an ideal basis of organization, where every one has an equal right to whatever comes to the common centre; where the centre itself becomes a radiating medium for the diffusion of the best of that which is brought to it, and where, all being freely given, no material considerations enter.

This is no ideal or imaginary picture. It is the simplest prose of every woman's club and every clubwoman's experience during the past thirty years.

It has been in every sense an awakening to the full glory and meaning of life. It is also a very narrow and self-absorbed mind that sees in these openings only opportunities for its own pleasure, or chances for its own advancement on its own narrow and exclusive lines. The lesson of the hour is help for those that need it, in the shape in which they need it, and kinship with all and everything that exists on the face of God's earth. If we miss this we miss the spirit, the illuminating light of the whole movement, and lose it in the mire of our own selfishness.

The tendency of association upon any broad human basis is to destroy the caste spirit, and this the club has done for women more than any other influence that as yet has come into existence. A club that is narrowed to a clique, a class, or a single object, is a contradiction in terms. It may be a society, or a congregation of societies, but it is not a club. The essence of a club is its many-sided character, its freedom in gathering together and expressing all shades of difference, its equal and independent terms of membership, which puts every one upon the same footing, and enables each one to find or make her own place. The most opposite ideas find equal claims to respect. Women widest apart in position and habits of life find much in common, and acquaintance and contact mutually helpful and advantageous. Club life teaches us that there are many kinds of wealth in the world—the wealth of ideas, of knowledge, of sympathy, of readiness to be put in any place and used in any way for the general good. These are given, and no price is or can be put upon them, yet they ennoble and enrich whatever comes within their influence.

We are only at the threshold of a future that thrills us with its wonderful possibilities—possibilities of fellowship where separation was; of love where hatred was; of unity where division was; of peace where war was; of light—physical, mental and spiritual—where darkness was; of agreement

and equality where differences and traditions had
built up walls of distinction and lines of caste.
This beautiful thing needs only to be realized in
thought to become an actual fact in life, and those
who do realize it are enriched by it beyond the
power of words to express.

Women have been God's own ministers everywhere and at all times.   In varied ways they have
worked for others until the name of woman stands
for the spirit of self-sacrifice.   Now He bids them
bind their sheaves and show a new and more
glorious womanhood; a new unit—the completed
type of the mother-woman, working with all as
well as for all.

The Advantages of a General Federation of Women's Clubs[1]

Address by Mrs. Croly to the First Meeting of the First Federation of Women's Clubs, Held in Brooklyn, N. Y., April 23, 1890

THE growth of the woman's club is one of the marvels of the last twenty-five years, so fruitful in the development of mental and material resources. What it was destined to become was, perhaps, far from the minds of those who aided its inception, but all the possibilities of the future lay in the germ that was thus planted, for it was formed by the marriage of two great elements—freedom and unity.

The club has been called the "school of the middle-aged woman." It is so in a very broad sense. It begins by gratifying her desire for fellowship, her thirst for knowledge; by training her in business and parliamentary methods; and gradually develops in her the power of expressing her own ideas, of concentrating her faculties and focusing them upon the object to be attained, the purpose to be accomplished. At the same time

[1] *The Cycle.*

she finds that a more subtle process has been going on in her own mind. An insensible alchemy has been widening her horizon, getting rid of prejudice, obliterating old, narrow lines, leaving in their place a willingness to see the good in Nazareth as well as in Galilee.

This result shows that she is a clubable woman, for it is emphatically the club spirit. It is in this respect that the club differs from those societies that are devoted to a single purpose; which demand subscription to an idea, an opinion, a dogma, a belief, a single basis or principle, and do not admit of fellowship on any other terms. Doubtless those have their uses — they are the necessary and often powerful expression of an advancing public opinion; but they have always existed, usually and in past times, under the leadership of men, even when composed of women. But it remained for the nineteenth century to develop a moral, social, and intellectual force, made up of every shade of opinion and belief, of every degree of rank and scholastic attainment, of every kind of disposition and habit of thought, all moulded into form,—and though as yet only the promise of what will be, furnishing an outline of that beautiful united womanhood which was the dream with which the club was started, and has been the guiding star to its development up to the present time.

The union of clubs in a federation is the natural

outgrowth of the club idea. It is the recognition of the kinship of all women, of whatever creed, opinion, nationality or degree; and it is a sign of a bond that entitles every one to equal place;—not to charity or toleration alone, but to consideration and respect. Inside of the club we are equal sharers of each other's gifts. Each one brings her knowledge, her sympathy, her special aptitude, her personal charm of manner and disposition, and we are all enriched by this outflowing and in-flowing, by this equal part and share in a foun-tain made up of such bountiful and diversified elements.

But the tendency of a circle is to widen. This is natural and necessary to healthful life. Stop its currents, dam up its inlets and outlets, and it is reduced to stagnation, and soon becomes foul and mischievous instead of healthy and life-giv-ing. The tendency of narrow ideas is to run to routine, to spend time and strength upon trivial details, and allow them to block and hinder the consideration of weightier matters. There is un-doubtedly a use for practice in business methods, particularly for those women who have had no previous training in business life; but the club ought to be an evolution. Once acquired, the knowledge of business ways, methods, and tactics can be put to better use than to aid or hinder the transaction of routine affairs, which it is the func-tion of a committee to dispose of.

The direction which the enlargement of club life takes must depend in the first place upon local conditions and environment. Already in many cities it has made itself, as in Philadelphia, the centre of the active, moral and intellectual forces. In others, as in Milwaukee, by coöperation in spirit and practice, it has provided a home for literature and the arts. Whatever the woman's club does, is and ought to be done on the broadest human principles; for if it forgets this it ceases to be a club, and becomes merely a propaganda for the advancement of certain fixed and unchangeable ideas.

But its own life, no matter how broad, is not enough. Whatever is vital is social. This is why a club when it comes to understand its own powers and sources of life, wishes for the companionship, the sympathy, the fellowship, the shaking hands with other clubs. It is said that corporations have no soul: clubs have souls, and they call loudly for the enlargement of club sympathies, the discussion of knotty club questions, the affirmation by others of what have become club convictions, and mutual congratulations on club successes.

This is not all that a federation of clubs can accomplish, but it is enough for a starting point. It is the kindly, providential, sympathetic way in which we are always led from the smaller to the larger field of work. Just before descending

from a crest in the Sierras into the valley of the
Yosemite, you come suddenly upon a wonderful
view; it is called "Inspiration Point," and it is
like an open door, a revelation of the infinite, a
promise in one gleam of transcendent beauty, of
all the separate and divisible splendors that are
to follow.

This spirit of enlargement beckons us and leads
us to the formation of the Federated Union of
Clubs, and we cannot do better than follow its
guidance. We all need, clubs as well as individuals, encouragement and counsel; we need to
enlarge our knowledge of what other clubs are
doing, of their extent, of their objects, of their
ambitions. Above all, we need to enlarge our
sympathies, to cultivate sympathy by knowledge;
for our prejudices are born of ignorance, and we
rarely dislike what we intimately know. As
Charles Lamb said: "How can I dislike a man
if I know him? Do we ever dislike anything if
we know it very well?" With the growth of
clubs the purely personal characteristics of them
will disappear, or at least be subordinated to
larger aims; and it is in the prosecution of these
larger aims that the federation will find its
reasons for existence.

There is a vast work for clubs to do throughout
the country in the investigation of moral and social questions, in the reformation of abuses, in the
cultivation of best influences;—not the influence

of class or clique or party, but a wide, liberal-izing, educational influence which works for true goodness, for cleanliness, for order, for equal op-portunities, for the recognition of God in man and nature, in whatever stage of unfolding the Divine in us may happen to be.   It is in the last twenty-five years that village-improvement societies, first instigated by a woman—Miss Sallie Goodrich of Stockbridge, Mass.—have created a transforma-tion in whole townships, and so enhanced the value of property as to drive out the original in-habitants and change farming communities into fashionable summer resorts.   This result is of doubtful value.   But every woman's club, espe-cially in the newer sections, has in its power, by wise and careful action, to improve the conditions, elevate the tone, and crystallize the moral force of its community in such a way as to make it more desirable to live in, more beneficial to its own citizens, more of an example to others.

All these questions of club life and work would naturally come up before a federated body, and these would as naturally lead to governmental questions; to contrasts and records of activities in different parts of the world, and to the investiga-tion of the causes which bring about certain results.

Women are naturally both receptive and con-structive.   The affirmative states of mind are those which particularly belong to women; as iconoclasts they are mere echoes. This affirmative condition is most favorable to true development. Nothing good has ever come of mere negation. But we must look for our truths and our basis of true growth, in the light of the rising dawn—not, as heretofore, in the waning glory of the setting sun. The union of clubs is the natural outgrowth of the planting of the true club idea. It was a little seed, but it contained the germ of a mighty growth in the kinship of all women— the women who differ as well as the women who agree; and the federation of clubs is the forerunner of that unity of the race of which philosophers have spoken, of which poets have dreamed, but which only the constructive motherhood and womanhood of the race can accomplish.

The Clubwoman[1]

THE nineteenth century has been remarkable in many ways. It has developed a new material and social order; but the fact is not as yet fully recognized that it has developed a new woman— the woman who works with other women; the woman in clubs, in societies; the woman who helps to form a body of women; who finds fellowship with her own sex, outside of the church, outside of any ism, or hobby, but simply on the ground of kinship and humanity.

It is not yet twenty-one years since a great daily in New York said that if a society composed wholly of women could hold together one year, a great many men would have to revise their opinion of women. The remark was made apropos of the formation of the first women's clubs in this country, and was echoed on all sides publicly and privately. It is only significant now as showing the isolated position of women, and the general impression which prevailed that they could not and would not work together, except, perhaps, for some common cause, religious or philanthropic, which for the time being absorbed their

[1] *The Cycle.*

energies and made them lose sight of their personal jealousies and animosities. Why women should have been believed to be antagonistic to women it is hard to say. This idea seems to have been cultivated assiduously by men, and women have echoed it; for it cannot be denied that the new fellowship that has come with the century and with the awakening of women to the life which is theirs—the life of friendship, of sympathy, of enlargement, of interest in affairs, of common kinship with all that exists in a beautiful world—has in it something of the nature of a surprise. Is it possible that women may have a life of their own, may learn to know and honor each other, may find solace in companionship, and lose sight of small troubles in larger aims?

These questions have been answered by thousands of women, answered with tears, after the manner of women, but tears of joyful recognition of the new day which has dawned for them;—a day of larger opportunities, a day which comes after a night of ages; for the woman is for the first time finding her own place in the world. Heretofore she was only welcome if the man wanted her, and if he no longer wanted her she was again cast out. But she is now learning that the world exists for her also; that she is one half the human race; that life, liberty, and the pursuit of whatever is good are as desirable for her as for the man, and as necessary in order to put her in *rapport* with the eternal springs of all life and its varied forms of activity.

The first impulse of the awakened woman is to unite herself with other women; her next to learn that which she does not know in regard to art, literature, peoples, races; the countries she has never visited, the kinsmen and kinswomen she has never seen, and the degree in which their progress has kept pace with or gone beyond her own. This knowledge comes to her through her club or literary society.

The woman's club has become the school of the middle-aged woman. It has brought her up to the time. It has enabled her to keep pace with the better advantages given to her sons and daughters. It has put an interest into her life which it had never previously possessed, and made her more humanly companionable because better able to judge and more willing to suspend judgment. The clubs of women in America—the growth mainly of the past twenty years—can now be counted by the hundreds, and their membership by many thousands, and the history of them all is practically the same.

It is this woman, born of women's clubs, who is the woman of to-day. She is the centre of the intellectual activity of townships and neighborhoods all over the country. She forms stock companies, and builds athenæums; she is at the head of working guilds; she organizes classes, teaches what she knows, while she is being taught what she did not know; and in mental activity, and labor which is not routine, has renewed her youth, and added to her attractions. She is at the same time far removed from a lobbyist. She is able to look at different sides; she is socially at home with the best people in every sense of the word. She is a lady as well as a woman, and does not adopt what is *outre* in order to obtain notoriety.

The New Life[1]

IT is a very dull mind, whether belonging to man or woman, that does not feel stirred by recent movements—not here alone but all over the world—into some quickening sense of the deeper life, the broader human claims, the unifying and uniting influences which have sprung into activity, and which address, not the visionary, but the thoughtful and far-seeing, with prophetic gleams of a new heaven and a new earth.

It is also a very narrow and self-absorbed mind which only sees in these openings opportunities for its own pleasure, or chances for its own advancement on its own narrow and exclusive lines. The lesson of the hour is help for those that need it, in the shape in which they need it, and kinship with all and everything that exists on the face of God's green earth. If we miss this, we miss the spirit, the illuminating light of the whole movement, and lose it in the mire of our own selfishness. To women this uplifting, these open doors, mean more than to men. They have been hedged about with so many restrictions, forced and held in such blind and narrow ways, that it is little

[1] *The Cycle.*

wonder if sight and steps are feeble, and that they
find it impossible to take it all in, or to recognize
at once the full meaning of the day that is dawn-
ing for them.

For we are only at the threshold of a future that
thrills us with its wonderful possibilities;—possibilities of friendship where separation was; of love
where hatred was; of unity where division was;
of peace where war was; of light—physical, mental and spiritual—where darkness was; of agreement and equality where differences and traditions
had built up walls of distinction and lines of caste.
This beautiful thing needs only to be realized in
thought to become an actual fact in life, and those
who do realize it are enriched by it beyond the
power of words to express. "I should like to
wake up rich one morning just to see how it
would feel," said one woman to another not long
since. "I do wake up rich every morning now,"
said the other, "though I have still my living to
earn, because my life is full of prized opportunities, of cherished friendships, of chances for ac-
quiring knowledge that I had not in youth, and
keeping myself in touch with broad human facts
and forces. Everything is interesting to me, more
interesting the closer my acquaintance with it, so
that I am fast getting rid of those ugly things we
call prejudices, and laying in a stock of appreciation instead, which is in itself enriching."

The old feeling of patron and dependant—so

irksome, so humiliating, so feudal, yet containing
for many the whole moral law — is done away
with, and in its place appears a spirit of true fellowship, a growing sense of mutual respect and
helpfulness. Club life teaches us that there are
many kinds of wealth in the world—the wealth
of ideas, of knowledge, of sympathy, of readiness
to be put in any place and used in any way for the
general good. These are given, and no price is
or can be put upon them; yet they ennoble and
enrich whatever comes within their influence.

Money is the only kind of wealth that is not
common, that is not given freely; and for that
reason it has a deadening and demoralizing effect
upon the minds of those who cultivate and in-
crease it for its own sake, or fail to put it to its
larger and more human uses. Wise distribution
is the only way in which money can be made
valuable in the world: it is only as a developing
power, as an aid to the worker, and a creator of
instrumentalities by which good objects can be
accomplished, that it is desirable. In the light of
this view, what place do those men and women
occupy who shut themselves up with their money,
and shut out the wide human interests which educate the mind and heart to noble issues? Going
to church does not help them, for it must be an
exclusive church and an exclusive pew, under an
exclusive pastor who patronizes Jesus Christ but
does not sympathize with Him, and who talks

about the " dregs of society " as if it were something fa. removed from the knowledge and consciousness of his hearers.

The woman of the past has especially been cramped up, bound around, and blindfolded by her special form of belief, by her tradition, by her social customs, by her education, by her whole environment; and the effect will remain stamped more or less upon her individuality long after the predisposing causes have passed away and better influences and circumstances have taken their place.

But the present is full of encouragement. The new life has begun: the woman is here;—not the martyred woman of the past; not the self-absorbed woman of the present, but the awakened woman of the future. That woman whose faculties have been cultivated, whose gifts have been trained, whose mind has been enlarged, whose heart-beats respond to the touch of the unseen human, and whose quickened insight recognizes father, brother, sister, and friend beneath the strange as well as the dilapidated robe.

This woman whose face no artist has painted, who is not yet familiar, is among us, and will remain. Her work humanizes and reconciles, and the changes it will effect will come so noiselessly that the majority will not be aware of them till they are accomplished, and then each one will announce, and perhaps believe, that they themselves

have brought these things about. But this will
not matter, for when the work is done it is
really of little consequence who did it, since all
who do any good work at all are simply agents
and ministers, charged with a task it is their business to perform, and happy only as they are able
to execute it. It is those who are " let alone,"
who live for and in themselves, who are the unhappy ones; and for these, though they possess
fine houses, much gold, stocks and bonds, the
poorest worker may well fervently pray that **the**
new life may come to these also.

The Days That Are[1]

WE live in an age of discontent. Discontent has been deified. It has been called divine; and unrest, the seal as well as the sign of progress. Doubtless there is a time and a place even for discontent, for there is no faculty that has not its function. But discontent, which is a sacred fire when it burns within and is kept for home use, is a mischievous and destroying element when it is widely distributed and unthinkingly employed by ignorance and short-sightedness.

Then it is certain that if discontent is good, content is far better, and thankfulness better yet. If time teaches us anything, it is to work and wait and trust; to be thankful for what is—for the digging and seeding time as well as for the harvest; for one must come before the other.

Time brings only one regret—that we had not more joy in the things that were; more belief, more patience, more love; more knowledge of the way things work out; more willingness to help toward the final result. The preparation, the planting, the laying foundations, must be done in

[1] *The Cycle.*

133

the dark; usually done with blind eyes as well,
which see not what may or will be, but anticipate
a harvest of pain from a spring-time of rain. Yet
these showers may have been indispensable to the
ground, and the seed may have expanded and
sent its shoots up to the surface in consequence
of them.

But why use symbols? The days that are;—
the days that are with us are the good days.
Suppose it is hard work, and only the prospect of
hard work? Work is the best thing we have got:
it is salvation. It is the means by which we
struggle up out of the darkness into the light. It
is the law of life. It is the ministry of all that is
good in the world; and the better it is the better
for us, the better for every one. It is only those
who do not know how to work that do not love it;
to those who do, it is better than play — it is
religion.

But this is the mere influence of work itself.
Suppose, besides your work, you have the blessing
of a family to be cared for, and your work provides
for them? This consecrates every part of it. It
makes every movement of the hand a benediction,
every heart-throb an unuttered prayer. Are not
these days so full of labor best days? For about
you are those you love. They are under the roof
you provide; their voices furnish the music, their
presence the sunshine of your life. Sometimes
that which your discontent craves will come to

you. The freedom from toil, the absence of "troubles" that now loom up so large to you; but with your troubles your joys will have vanished, and you will sit in the twilight waiting for the end, and wishing that you had cultivated the sweetness instead of the bitterness of the beginning, that you had not allowed the thorns to cover up your roses.

Wisdom seems to have been the same always, but each one has to learn its lessons for himself. That is the reason why there is so little apparent progress in essential truths. There are always those who have grown into their realization; there are always those who are at the threshold, and who must travel over the same paths, for we can none of us acquire true wisdom for another; it must become a part of ourselves of our own moral and spiritual consciousness.

"It is all very well for you," says one; "you have never known the pinch of poverty." How do you know that? We none of us know how and where the shoe has pinched another person's foot. It is not our business to know, but it is our business to prevent our soreness from becoming sourness and bitterness. It is our business to make the pathway of others as pleasant as we can, so that their unseen corns shall irritate them as little as possible. All the wisdom of the days that have been, and the days that are, will be found in the following lines from Goethe's "Tasso":

"Would'st thou fashion for thyself a seemly life?
    Then fret not over what is past and gone;
    And spite of all thou mayest have lost behind,
    Yet act as if thy life were just begun.
    What each day wills, enough for thee to know,
    What each day wills, the day itself will tell.
    Do thine own task, and therewith be content;
    What others do that shalt thou fairly judge.
    Be sure that thou no mortal brother hate,
    Then all beside leave to the Master Power."

A People's Church[1]

"WHAT would you do if you were rich?" This is a question often asked, and readily answered by those who have not wealth of their own to dispose of, for there is nothing easier than to give away other people's money. But it is more difficult to the conscientious, who feel that their unearned millions ought to inure in some way to the public benefit, yet do not always see the way to the reconciling of their own conditions and circumstances with that use of money which seems to them wisest and best.

As a rule it may safely be assumed that if all who are poor were suddenly made rich, they would do as the majority of our rich men do with their money—keep it. But it is at least pleasant to think how generous one might be, and as the rich occasionally are; and I propose to suggest one object that I hope will one day be realized in this great city, where everything good is possible, as well as everything evil, and which only needs to take vital root in some active mind to become a living reality.

Within a certain area New York may be called a city of churches, but they are churches for the

[1] *The Cycle.*

137

rich; solemn, imposing, cathedral-aisled, glass-stained, costly, munificently beneficed, elegantly pastored—God locked in, the poor locked out. I know there are "mothers'" meetings and "mite" societies, and all the rest of it, but all the same the poor woman in her old shawl and bonnet would not think of entering one of those expensive pews, nor does the man in his working suit feel that that is the place for him. Outside, the majority of churches take no account of the necessity for the consolation, the comfort, the upbuilding, the refreshment of religion, save and only for certain hours on Sunday, and then it must be in full toggery, and in company with the eminently respectable.

The most beautiful thing about the old churches abroad is not their splendor of carving and painting, but that they stand with open doors week days and Sundays, for the people to enter; and they do enter. The market woman with her basket drops in for a moment on her way home from the labor of her weary day. The old woman totters in to say her " Ave Maria," the young woman to pray away her perplexities. Even the business man sometimes finds it a resource from his struggles and temptations. The poor, with their crowded houses and narrow quarters, have so little privacy as to make quiet, and even an opportunity for self-communion, a luxury. Then how often in the perplexities which fill their lives they desire for a little while a retreat, a refuge where they can think, perhaps receive a word of counsel, at least find an atmosphere of absolute peace and restfulness.

The Monday prayer-meeting, the afternoon exhortation; the evening conference of the Baptists, the Methodists, the Presbyterians, or the Congregationalists, are not what is wanted; nor is it a cold and barn-like edifice which makes one feel, if one goes to call upon God, as though He were out, and could only be seen at stated times, and by the will of the sexton and the trustees.

A people's church is wanted, where the people can come and go as they please; which asks no questions, which is always open, which has brief singing and organ services that all and any people of any kind and degree may attend and feel themselves welcome. A morning service of praise, a mid-day song of rejoicing, a vesper hymn of thankfulness. No word of condemnation, no word of controversy, no word of doubt, no word of assertion or denial; only unceasing love, continued and eternal recognition of human kinship and readiness to minister to any soul's need as far as it may be reached and helped.

No one minister could perform its offices; its servants would have to be in a manner consecrated to its work, and they should be men and women who have suffered, and therefore know, but who would find more reason for rejoicing than

lamentation; who would possess gifts of music
and oratory, and whose personal influence would
be strong for righteousness.

There are great churches with scattered congregations, in Fifth avenue; there are a few poor
churches, and small, for which no one cares, and
which offer no attractions to the over-flowing
population of Mott street. The spring and summer will soon come, and then these great churches
will be closed, their pew-owners distributed over
lake and mountain in all the different parts of the
wide world. But the "people" will be here.
People who work in foundries and shops, who live
in tenement-houses; people who earn a hand-
to-mouth living as clerks, book-keepers, seam-
stresses and petty store-keepers; people who
have to stay in such homes as they can support
because they cannot afford to break them up and
go elsewhere.

For these people and their children there is only
the street. The children occupy the street. For
four or five months in the year they make life
hideous, especially on Sunday, by noise and ex-
hibition of vandalism that would disgrace the
savages of any age or nation. The police acknowledge themselves powerless to prevent it. It
is simply the exercise of undirected faculty which
might be turned to account, but which has only
noise, confusion, and street warfare for its opportunity for exercise.

There are possibilities in these congregations of the highways and byways, and when we have our people's church or churches, open all the year, and all the night as well as all the day, and the voices of the angels for sweetness, singing love and peace on earth, in an anthem that pierces the roof, and with the tones of a mighty organ to emphasize to all the world its message, and it is not a question of clothes, many people will be glad to listen, and will find an influence in the music, in the willingness, in the free-heartedness, in the sympathy, in the kindness, in the spirit of brotherhood, that they would not get out of preaching nor dogma.

Whom are we waiting for to build this church? Is it a woman? Surely it is an opportunity that carries the two-fold blessing.

Notes, Letters and Stray Leaves

Notes, Letters and Stray Leaves

A " FREE LANCE " is less free than the organs of a party. In one case it means at least the opinions of a group; in the other, the dogmatism of the one who wields the lance. Nothing is less free than the self-styled freedom of the individual.

Enthusiasm implies a certain narrowness of vision. When people can take a broad view they can see the elements of goodness or beauty everywhere, and they cease to be enthusiastic in regard to one. The great popular preachers are not university men, or those who are quiet and literary in style, but strong, dogmatic men.

Perhaps the most noticeable difference between the so-called new woman and the new man is this, that she is seizing every opportunity that opens up new avenues of individual employment, while he is discovering and storing energy to save himself from doing any work at all. The old man made other men, and women too, work for him, the new man is making the hitherto uncontrolled forces his servants, locking them up in such small compass that a twist of the wrist will start the crash of worlds.

The notes of the great god Pan, so " piercingly sweet by the river "—a far cry and a weary way from Pan to Handel and Beethoven; yet during all that time music has been the joy and the consolation of peoples,—all except the Quakers.

If Poetry is the prophet of the future, music expresses all emotions,—love, joy, fear, above all, aspiration.   Music is essentially religious, and has inspired the most perfect forms of emotional composition we know.

I take off my hat to the new man — that is, I would if I wore one, but I wear a bonnet, and pin it on with long, sharp-pointed things which if they were not used voluntarily would be considered instruments of torture.   Think of the man who is testing the force of dynamite—who is holding lightning bolts in his hand and forcing them to do the work which he has planned for them, who is taking the altitude of the mountains in Mars in his observatory in the air at midnight,— think of these men stopping to swear while they ran the murderous little weapon through six thicknesses of buckram, lining, velvet, lace, feathers, ribbon and hair — to fasten on their bonnets!

October, 1900.

MY DEAR FRIENDS AND FELLOW-MEMBERS:

It was really a grief to me not to be able to meet you individually and collectively before leaving to be absent the entire season. The accident which disabled me for the summer, threatens to cripple me for the winter also, and in this condition of dependence and general disability, it seemed best to go where I could have seclusion, and the care of some member of my own family.

I resign my place among you with less reluctance because the Woman's Press Club is now strong and well able to guard its own interests, and direct its own affairs. It will, I am sure, be all the better and stronger from being thrown upon its own resources, and made to depend wholly upon the potent efforts which have been evoked, and which may be still further developed on the part of its membership.

It will be a source of the deepest satisfaction to me in my retirement to think of you in connection with the happy times we have had, and the good work done during the past three years, and also of the spirit of loving fellowship which has grown so strong and so deep. Nothing can give greater pleasure than to hear of your continued growth and prosperity, of continued endeavor to make the work effective, and the life of the Woman's Press Club beautiful and useful.

Remember that a well-rounded club is an epitome of the world; that it never can and never ought to be perfect according to any one individual's idea of perfection, for every one's ideal is different; and it is the unity in this diversity which constitutes the spiritual life of the club, as the soul animates and inspires the body.

Exalt the club. Bring your best to the front. Extinguish personal aims. Mind not at all the little picking and carping of human gadflies, whose desire to extract blood is perhaps a survival of their species, and an evidence of their unfitness for human companionship.

I think of you at every gathering, and if you remember me, show it in your determination to make the Woman's Press Club of Greater New York an honor to the metropolis of the New World and to American womanhood.

J. C. CROLY.

HILL FARM, HERSHAM,
    WALTON-ON-THAMES, ENGLAND.

Letter to Sorosis

May, 1899.

TO MY DEAR FRIENDS AND FELLOW-MEMBERS
OF SOROSIS:

On the eve of my departure from New York for a season, my heart turns towards Sorosis with a depth of affection I find it difficult to put into words. For thirty years it has held a large place in my life. It has represented the closest companionship, the dearest friendships, the most serious aspirations of my womanhood. The past is filled with delightful memories, social and intellectual, of which it was the happy instrument and inspiration. Its galleries are stored with living pictures of noble women who were with us, who are always of us, who have become a part of that eternal source of spiritual life from which the best things spring. What is the secret of the strength of Sorosis? What is its value to the community and the world at large? It is, as a centre of unity. This is our Holy Grail,—and this we are bound never to defame, or defile by thought, word or deed.

We planted the seed not in Sorosis alone, but in the General Federation; and it is our duty to see that it is preserved in its integrity. Sorosis does not want place or power in the organization she created, but it is hers to see that the great principle it embodied is not lost sight of. That the limitless growth and expansion provided for in its foundations are always from centre to circumference, not in sections; and that as differences are not recognized in the local organization, so there can be no north, south, east, or west in the general organization, nor any separation or division of interests. This is the aim of Sorosis:—to perfect within its own membership that unity in diversity which is the basis of its life, and the source of its growth; and, as far as its strength and influence extend, preserve it as the foundation of a united womanhood.

The consolation I feel in going away is that I shall find you here when I return; not, I hope, crippled and disabled as now, but able to be among you once more. I leave a monument of the woman's club in the " Women's Club History," which carries marvellous testimony to the ideals and aspirations of the woman of the home —for this is the woman of the club.

God bless and keep you all! I wish I could look into your kind faces individually, and thank you for all that Sorosis past and present has been to me.

Faithfully yours,

J. C. CROLY.

Letter to the Society of American
Women in London

November, 1901.

TO THE SOCIETY OF AMERICAN WOMEN IN
  LONDON:

On the eve of my departure for America, I desire to express to the Society of American Women something of what I feel sure I owe it individually and collectively since its initial gathering in the beginning of March.

My visit to England has been made under extremely trying and painful circumstances. I had expected no participation in any social functions. I had communicated with only a very few near and dear friends. Formal intercourse with comparative strangers seemed impossible.

But there was nothing strange in the atmosphere of the American Society. It provided at once an atmosphere in which one could breathe freely, so kindly and so cordial were its tone and spirit.

It formed at once a social centre in which the best elements contributed to the most varying attractions. It brought together many of the most charming and progressive women in English as well as American society, and also many of the brilliant women we read about, but rarely meet.

In addition, it performed a most useful office in

extending the hand of welcome from American women in London to the representative women who attended the International Council; and has a future of exceptional character in filling a social need which has never been filled by the official representatives in republican America.

It is not too much to say that it has put life in London in quite a new and much more attractive aspect to American women, by focusing the best elements and bringing them in touch with each other. With time and development the highest results of the modern co-operative spirit should be attained, and the fulness of a life that will enrich each individual member, and reach out beyond to an ever widening sphere of happy influence.

J. C. CROLY.

Letter to the Pioneer Club of London

June, 1901.

TO THE FINANCE COMMITTEE OF THE PIONEER
    CLUB:

I hope I shall not be considered as taking a liberty in presenting a subject of some importance for your consideration.

There is a feeling in some clubs and among some clubwomen that the time has arrived for expanding the club idea and at the same time drawing closer the ties which unite women in the form of organized fellowship, which the modern clubwoman recognizes as a potent and most valued element of her club life. It is believed, in short, that the time has come for the initial steps to be taken for the formation of a European Federation of Women's Clubs.

There are many reasons which seem to make it eminently proper that the Pioneer Club should be the one to take these initial steps. It is the oldest and best known woman's club in London. It was founded upon the broadest human lines by a woman who possessed in the highest degree that sixth sense which the nineteenth century contributes to the twentieth—the sense of the Universal. This led her to affiliate the Pioneer Club in the beginning with the General Federation of Women's Clubs in the United States, and should inspire it to progressive life and work.

The initial step is not formidable. It is, if thought desirable, simply to address a circular letter to women's clubs on record, wherever they may be known to exist, proposing a basis of federated affiliation, and inviting them to unite in forming a grand Federation of organized bodies of women capable of realizing any purpose upon which they might bring their united forces to bear.

If it is said, " Of what use is such a Federation?" I might point to many instances of educational and municipal progress, and social reform

154 JANE Cunningham Croly

in America effected by this combined effort.   But details are as nothing compared with the one great, glowing, ultimate aim of the solidarity of thoughtful, high-minded, intelligent, progressive women.   It is written in the stars.   It will surely become an accomplished fact; and there are other clubs willing to take the initiative; but it is fitting that the Pioneer Club should lead, and by its wisdom and judgment lend an added dignity to noble endeavor.

J. C. CROLY.

Letters to Mrs. Dimies T. S. Denison, President of Sorosis

22 AVENUE ROAD,
LONDON, N W., January 27, 1899.

MY DEAR MRS. DENISON:

Thank you very much for your delightful letter. It was so good and heartening.   Its spirit was so representative of the best that club-life has given us that it made me feel more than ever thankful for Sorosis and for that reserved strength and all-roundedness of resource and character which makes it able to successfully tide over any difficulties.

I have not heard of any effort to form a London Sorosis, nor do I think it could be done successfully on precisely the same lines.   If we were starting a club to-day it would differ considerably

from the one started thirty-one years ago.   That
had to be formed out of such materials as were
available at that time, and built as it knew and
as it grew.   Its virtue lay in its breadth, in the
true and scientific character of its conception.   It
made a centre and worked from that to the radiating points of an illimitable circle, not knowing
precisely where these would take it, but with all
the faith of Columbus in results founded upon
essential principles.   We had no idea at the time,
that at every one of these farther points other cen-
tres were being formed that also, in their own time
and way, struck out feelers and shafts, and thus
became part of that great system of creative force,
which, still acting on its central and original idea
of a larger unity, brought together the General
Federation.   This is the mother idea which Sorosis represents, and which needs no legal enact-
ment to enforce.   It stands for this as much in
London as in New York, and in its own way has
become unique.   It lacks some of the elements of
the newer clubs, but it contained the germ of them
all, and is essentially a true growth, an aggrega-
tion of all the qualities of a diverse and unified
womanhood;—not by making it something else,
but by studying its own spirit and life, and the
genius it has developed.

First, it stands for a wide hospitality and the
generous recognition of all other women; for high
standards in literature, art, ethics, and all the

interests belonging to and growing out of them. Above all, it stands for home duty; for honor, faithfulness, loyalty, courage and truth. Finally, it stands for subjection;—that highest subjection of the one will to the many; of that subordination of our own dominant desire to the spirit and will of God, represented by the spirit and will of the majority. For the voice of the people is in a real sense the voice of God, whether we recognize it or not.

O my beloved Sorosis, you are the core of my heart! What have I said but that you represent an ideal of life and character, and that each member should hold herself responsible for its preservation and its increasing beauty and value?

Faithfully yours,
J. C. CROLY,
Honorary President.

DEAREST MRS. DENISON: When I began this letter it was intended for you alone; as I went on it seemed as if it might find a little place at the Breakfast. Use your own judgment in regard to having an extract made for that purpose. . . .

Yours lovingly,   J. C. C.

QUEEN'S ROAD, ST. JOHN'S WOOD,
LONDON, N. W., April 16, 1899.

MY DEAR PRESIDENT:

What a lovely programme! I am so proud to show it, and so happy that Sorosis is going on so beautifully. Have I congratulated you? If not, let me do it now with all my heart. I always knew your time would come, and that you would make a popular as well as a wise president. You have a light touch, but a very appreciative one, and that good thing—a fine sense of humor. You do not take yourself too seriously, but you give the best of yourself unreservedly. God bless you for carrying the banner of Sorosis up to its highest level, and maintaining its dignity in a way worthy of its reputation.

The London Club, or Society of American Women in London, is flourishing. The president comes often to see me, and in her address at the second luncheon, April 10th, said that she considered it a special providence that I was in London at the beginning; that I had been of the greatest help to her, and that she should always look upon me as their " Club Mother." I began to wonder if that was what my leg was broken for, and how many more times I might have to be cut to pieces to make " Mother " enough to go around.

Mrs. Henry Norman (Muriel Dowie, author of " A Girl in the Carpathians ") made a brilliant little speech. She is delightful, and very anxious to visit America. Her husband is the Englishman who of his own choice graduated from Harvard. He has written some very appreciative articles about America. . . .

I hope I shall know when Mrs. F. and Mrs. L. are coming, and something of their plans. At least how long they will stay in London. Won't you be so good as to tell them this and give them my address?

I am endeavoring now to put myself under treatment for the pain and weakness I feel when I try to walk (with sticks) in the street. . . .

Really yours,

J. C. CROLY.

7 RUE D'ASSAS, PARIS, FRANCE,
October 3, 1900.

MY VERY DEAR PRESIDENT AND FRIEND:

Your letter was most welcome. I have been in a quiet little country place since coming from Ober-Ammergau, and know no one. I thought much of you in those quiet days, and wished to write, but waited to hear, and the echoes did come in a way I understood, for I had letters before leaving America which were an indication of the general trend of thought and desire. Of course I never for a moment misunderstood your attitude in the matter of the election. . . . You could not help your election. [Referring to the first vice-presidency of the General Federation.]

I am very, very sorry the color question has been raised again. It almost made a split six years ago. It was, at the best, premature. It was a sacrifice of the greater to the less, of the real good we had attained and the ideal towards which we were working, to a theoretical possibility which had not yet presented itself. We have yet a thousand obstacles to overcome within ourselves; a thousand problems to solve; an ideal to work towards capable of infinite expansion. But we should not strain the limits while the centre still lacks order and form, and depends upon the wisdom with which it is guided for permanence.

We have made some dreadful blunders, . . . but ideals are not stones in the street; they are stars in the sky. They are always beyond us; we cannot wear them as breast-pins but we can work towards them. . . .

Yours faithfully,
J. C. CROLY.

82 GOWER STREET, BEDFORD SQUARE,
LONDON, W. C., April 10, 1901.

MY VERY DEAR FRIEND AND PRESIDENT:

How good it was of you to send me the beautiful souvenirs of the thirty-third Annual Breakfast. They took me straight back to you all through a mist of tears that were half pleasure, half pain; pleasure that I was not forgotten, pain that I was not there to see the loving glance, and share the hand-clasp. It is true I have many friends here, but none that seem quite like the old friends; and there is only one Sorosis—God's blessing be upon

it for evermore!   Yet wherever I go, God's blessing and His Spirit seem to me to have descended
upon women.   They show the most wonderful
goodness and insight.   They seem each one to be
specially made; not the kind that are kept in
stock, so to speak.   Oh, I feel sometimes as if all
my life had been partly a test, partly an experience of their goodness, and that it is a sufficient
blessing, for nothing else has been left me.

A writer remarked the other day, in an article
on the South African war, that the best results of
war were ties—the spirit of good comradeship that
it established among men.   This is what we pre-
eminently get out of our club life, and without
paying so fearful a price for it.   I hope to see you
all when you come together in the autumn.

With loving remembrance,

J. C. CROLY.

Letters to Mrs. Charlotte Carmichael Stopes (London)

11 BARTON STREET, WEST KENSINGTON,
Jan. 15, 1889.

MY DEAR MRS. STOPES:
It is very kind of you to take this trouble to
give us a pleasure, and I would not miss it on
any account.   But it is a little difficult for me to
name the day.   I am in the hands of the dentist

this week; I shall hardly get through to go to the Writers' Club on Friday. These two circumstances have postponed my visit to Miss Genevieve Ward to whom it is now arranged that I go a week from to-morrow. I could make it any afternoon that week that would suit you. Mrs. Sidney will be delighted also to accept your invitation; and perhaps Miss Ward also. Please make the afternoon to suit yourself and Miss Blackburn.

Really yours,
J. C. CROLY.

Jan. 19.

I go to Miss Ward's on Monday. It is her day at home, and therefore will be more or less fatiguing. Tuesday I have promised to dine at the Crescent Club with Mrs. Phillips and hear Mr. Felix Moscheles' lecture afterwards. Miss Ward and her brother, Col. Albert Lee Ward, go also. Three days of continuous going out would be too much for me, and something would have to give way. I would rather it would be any event than yours. Suppose you arrange it for the week following, and in the meantime call for me at Miss Ward's on Monday. You will find Miss Ward a very striking personality, and I particularly wish Col. Ward to accompany me to your house. I will see you on Friday, and you can tell me how you decide.

J. C. CROLY.

Friday the 27th will suit me very well. I have been out-of-doors so little as yet, that I feared I might break down on the third day of trying. I do know Lady Roberts Austen; have been to luncheon at her house, but have not seen her since I came this time; I have communicated as yet with so few. I heard from her the other day however, and I know she will go to your house if she possibly can. I have to drive wherever I go. I move too slowly for crowds and public conveyances. I cannot risk weather.

Feb. 8.

I want to thank you for the afternoon I spent at your house; I enjoyed it so very much. You will not consider me " pushing " if I say I am only half satisfied. There are so many sides to your house; I want to see the Queen of Scots portrait again, and the Donatello, and some of your rare cookery books. I expect to change my quarters in about three weeks to the North West; then you will let me come and browse, won't you. But first you must come and lunch with me. With kind regards to your delightful family,

I am, etc.

March 12.

May I come up next Thursday afternoon and bring with me an American friend, Mrs. Stockber

of Silverton, Colorado, who has just arrived by
the *Umbria*. Mrs. Stockber is an unusually interesting woman. She is equal owner with her
husband, an intelligent and large-minded German, of one of the largest silver mines in the States,
and is one of the only two honorary women members of the great Association of Mining Engineers
of the United States. Mrs. Griffin, the President
of the new Society of American Women in London, also wants to come. I don't want to inundate
you; and this is only to ask if you are better, and
can receive a trio safely.

Yours, etc.

March 16.

I am sorry to give you so much trouble.
But I have a friend here just now, a woman of
unusual character and ability. I remember I told
you of her. The other is Mrs. Helen T. Richards
of the Boston Institute of Technology. The only
moment I can get her is on Monday afternoon,
and I want her to see the collection of prints and
your pictures. If it is all right I will bring her
with me on Monday at 3 P.M. We must go to Miss
Ward's at 4.30. Do not have tea at that primitive hour; for we shall be obliged to have a cup
at Miss Ward's. I wish we might have a chance
of seeing Mr. Stopes; but of course that is something that may be prayed for, but not what com-

mon people are made for.   Dear, take care of
yourself if you can.   There is only one of you.
Yours,

J. C. C.

March 17.

We will postpone.   I cannot reach my two
troublesome friends, and next week you will be
busy and tired.   " By-and-by " is coming with
the sun and flowers.   We will come too.
Yours lovingly and really,

J. C. C.

June 25, 1901,
82 Somers' Street, W. C.

My very dear Friend:

I have only time to thank you for your kind
" welcome," and tell you how sorry I am not to
see you to-day, and your precious Winnie, who I
hope has really started on the road to recovery.
Children are the richest boon vouchsafed us in
this world, and the parents are the trustees of this
wealth committed to their charge, but belonging
to the world at large, and of which time only tells
the value.   I shall be very busy now for a few
days, but will see you as soon as possible.
Affectionately,

J. C. C.

, Remember that a
-rounded club is an
of the world. That
never can, and never

5 to be perfect
to any one individual's
idea of perfection;
every one's ideal is
and it is the unity in
diversity which constitut
the spiritual life of
Club; as the soul
and inspires the body.

Exalt the club. Bring your best to the front. Extinguish arms. Mind not at a the little picking, carping of human q whose desire to extract is perhaps a survival of species; and an evidence their unfitness for companionship.

Jenny June C.
Hill Farm
Hersham; Walton-on-

222 WEST 23D STREET,
NEW YORK, Jan. 16, 1901.

MY DEAR FRIEND:

Thank you very much for your letter and card. It was a great pleasure to me to receive it, and to learn something about yourself and what you are doing. The news was long belated. The letter was to have been printed the week that I left, and I provided to have it sent to about a dozen friends as a good-bye. But it was so long delayed by Transvaal excitement and sad war news, that I did not expect it to appear at all.

I had a wonderful celebration on my seventieth birthday in December; poems written, cakes with seventy candles sent, and a great spontaneous gathering in my honor, which really bothered me not a little, for I do not pose worth a cent, and do not know where to look or what to do when people compliment me.

However, one thing gratified me above all others. It was a "birthday party" given me by the Daughters of 1812—the most exclusive of patriotic societies that is restricted to lineal descendants. The gathering was magnificent; the cake was brought in lighted by seventy candles borne on the shoulders of four men. By unanimous vote they conferred upon me honorary membership, and the insignia were conferred. The president in seconding the motion said, this departure from their rules (alluding to my English birth) was not in honor of " the club," nor of the " literary women," but of the woman who knew no line of separation, and whose work had been done for all women. Was not that a beautiful thing to say? Only that I intend to be cremated, I would have it put on my tombstone.

We had a very bright and very beautiful beginning here to the " Holy Year," so far as weather is concerned, and it is also very gay, though my lameness prevents me from participating much in social doings. I am also grieved by the unexpected effects of the Boer war, in England. There must have been shocking blundering and mismanagement somewhere. The pitying way in which " poor, stupid, decrepit old England " is talked about is galling. Some military officers remarked recently that England was hardly worth having a " scrap " with, she would be so easy to beat.

Our General Federation holds a Congress in Paris in June, and my passage is taken for May 19th. If nothing untoward prevents, I shall be in London for a week early in June, and then go to Paris and Ober-Ammergau. If you could go it would be very pleasant. Give my love to your daughters, and kind regards to Mr. Stopes.

Yours ever,

J. C. CROLY.

Letter to Mrs. Carrie Louise Griffin

82 GOWER STREET, BEDFORD SQUARE, W. C.
June 25, 1901.

MY DEAR MRS. GRIFFIN:

Mr. Bell wants an article immediately, about the American Society, for the Chicago *Recorder;* and I am glad to write it, because it enables me to make it stand for what it does; and will, still more, in the very heart of western clubdom; and will be a John the Baptist for you if you should go over next summer. He wants some photographs, yours particularly; which please send. He left his card with address of *Recorder* in Fleet Street, which I omitted to take up-stairs at the moment, and afterwards it could not be found. I am hoping that you have it and will give it to me, or that Mr. Griffin perhaps knows it. If you can drop in on Monday, A.M., I should be glad to ask you in regard to some members—what to say of them, etc. Would Mrs. Clarence Burns allow her picture to be used, and have you one of Mrs. De Friese?

Always faithfully yours,

J. C. CROLY.

From a Letter to Mrs. May Riley Smith

. . . I have never done anything that was not helpful to woman so far as it lay in my power. (April 2, 1886.)

Letters to Miss Anna Warren Story (Chairman of Executive Committee of the Woman's Press Club of New York)

HILL FARM COTTAGE, HERSHAM,
WALTON-ON-THAMES, ENGLAND,
Oct. 29, 1900.

MY DEAR EXECUTIVE:

Your letter giving me all the news to date was most kind and welcome. It seems very strange to be away from you all in this secluded corner of Surrey, with nothing in sight but woods, a meadow in which cows are grazing, and one neighboring cottage. My morning walk, when the weather will admit of walking, is along the old post road lined with woods and at the foot of our little lane or entrance to farm. The other morning one solemn old cow put her head through the fence, and stared with amazement at my crutches. Four others walked over to see what she was looking at; and they all stood in a row, looking and making no sound as long as I could see them. It was very funny.

It seems so odd after so many years of continuous and often hurried work, to be using days for walking, and little things that since I was a grown woman have been crowded into odds and ends of time, or omitted for want of enough of it.

I am gaining strength, however, and realize how complete the prostration was, and how radical the reconstructive processes had to be. The seclusion in which I live, surrounded by pine woods, a mile and a half from the nearest post office (tho' a postman brings our letters) and an equal distance from such supplies as a village can afford, is a little trying in some ways, but a real boon to me in my present condition.

It would have been very easy to plunge into the activities of women in London. Many invitations have reached me, but I have been nowhere but to one little dinner given by our only neighbor, the wife of a London editor, and herself a popular story writer.

I can walk now with one crutch and a stick, and begin to hope for complete restoration, which at one time seemed to me impossible. But, oh, how tedious and wearing it is! We have an unusually fine October for England, but gray skies and almost daily rains now. But the Surrey country is beautiful, full of quaint old villages and objects of picturesque interest. I am longing for the time and the weather to explore it. I could write all day about my gradually growing desire to be " up and doing." But time and space do not admit. Let me say in one word how deeply I was touched by the action of the Executive Committee, the Governing Board, and club. But I am also disappointed. I wanted to leave the field clear, and have new energy put into the club by bringing into active and central circulation the young, best blood we possess. Thank you for your assurance that as far as possible that will be done; and thank every officer and every member in my behalf for the long and affectionate confidence they have reposed in me, and for the many acts of personal kindness I have received from them.

I am sorry you have lost the Countess by removal, and other valuable members by death. . . .

Yours faithfully and affectionately,

J. C. CROLY.

NORFOLK VILLA, WEYBRIDGE, SURREY,
August 20, 1901.

MY DEAR ANNA:

Your letter came most opportunely. I had been thinking about you, the Press Club, and my dear friends at home; for somehow I have not felt the old pleasure in being in England, and if I had a home to come back to, and my goods and chattels were not so far off, I should have come back, I think, this autumn.

For one thing, the weather has not been favorable. We had such warm weather in July; but every month has had a week or more of very cold and wet weather. In Ober-Ammergau on the 8th of July we perished with the cold, and the rain almost caked in ice upon us. Still, even such weather could not spoil Ober-Ammergau. It is the one thing of its kind on earth, and the nearest to an absolutely perfect thing I ever saw. A great charm is the unconsciousness of the performers. They do not play to an audience. There are no footlights, nothing theatrical; only the Great Tragedy wrought out as a living reality. I think of all the scenes; the one that made the deepest impression upon me was the one in which there were the fewest actors and least acting. That was the Garden of Gethsemane. So intense was the agony of spirit, that it seemed as if I myself should cry out if the disciples had not gone away and left the Saviour alone to his mortal struggle.

It is a great thing, Anna, that these people have done. They have lived the Passion of Christ for nearly three hundred years. They are born in it; they are fed upon it. They have made a cult of religion; and they are absolutely religious, but not in the least sectarian. The Christ they have lifted up draws all men unto him.

I have been in a quiet country place for four weeks, and shall stay two weeks longer. . . . If I remain this winter we shall probably go back to Paris by November and to Italy in the spring. Now that I am here I might as well give myself this one more chance. . . . I was very tired when I came back from our hurried trip, and was very glad of rest and quiet. . . .

Do not let my dear friends in the Press Club build upon me, or weaken their force by re-electing me. Elect a young, strong, press woman. Anna, do this without any reference to personal feeling or likes or dislikes. You are capable of acting impersonally. Beg the club to do this in my name, and to pick out their best for the chairmen of their representative committees.

My own dear friends and fellow members; how I wish I could make them feel the strength of my desire for their growth in wisdom and honor. God bless them all!

Yours affectionately and faithfully,

J. C. CROLY.

ASHOVER, DERBYSHIRE,
May 30, 1901.

MY DEAR ANNA:

Your kind letter arrived this morning, forwarded by Mrs. Sidney to this remote village in Derbyshire. I left London ten days ago because I had to get fresh air and quiet. Ashover is a quiet little village; a paradise of meadows starred with flowers, and wooded and cultivated; hills in which all the treasures of one of the richest counties in England (in floral wealth) are to be found. When I came here there were still primroses, cowslips, violets, forget-me-nots, and fields white with small daisies and yellow with buttercups. Now there are masses of yarrow, marguerites, rhododendrons, bluebells, and great trees of white and purple lilacs. Roses, I am told, will cover everything by and by, but development is a little late this year. I wish you could spend a month here this summer: what a revelation of English beauty it would be to you!

Thank you for your sympathy with my personal troubles. I am not unhappy. . . . The goodness of women to me is always and everywhere miraculous. This alone makes life worth living. . . .

I am rejoiced to hear of the Press Club's prosperity. Nothing could give me greater pleasure than to know of its constant growth and advancement.

With love, ever yours,

J. C. CROLY.

Letters to Mrs. Caroline M. Morse

HILL FARM COTTAGE, WALTON-ON-THAMES,
SURREY, ENGLAND, Dec. 13, 1898.

MY DEAR FRIEND:

I was sorry to know from Ethel's note, received day before yesterday, that you had been ill, and were still unable to the task of writing. I wished above all things that I could in some way help and comfort you, having always in mind the help and comfort you were to me during the trying days last summer that followed my accident, and the consequent long and tedious illness. There are many people who feel sympathetically, but so few are capable and who are ready or are permitted to apply the act of sympathy. It is the friend in need that is the friend we remember with a grateful, lasting love. .   .   .

At this moment we are on the eve of removal to London where we are taking rooms once occupied by the family of David Christie Murray. We go to-morrow, and begin a new chapter in this most disastrous of years. So many things seem to culminate toward the close of the century—good fortune for some, evil fortune for others; hopes dashed at the seeming moment of realization, as if all the forces in nature were aiding to make an end of the century's efforts in any way that would bring finality.

For my part I feel as if I had been forcibly brought to a standstill. In a few days (the 19th) I shall have reached the milestone: I shall be seventy. Sorosis would have made an occasion of it if I had been in New York. As it is, I feel a little tinge of regret that my annihilation last June was not more complete; that I did not leave, along with my dear friend, Mrs. Demorest. Not that I am wholly unhappy; I only feel somehow brought to an unfinished close; left in a state of animated suspension. I seem to see everything from a distance; separated by my inability to participate in the goings and comings, the doings and pleasures of others. I feel the wall that stands between those who still live and those who have passed from this world; but alas, I still retain consciousness, and desire for sympathy, and can see and hear and feel, though my feet are chained.

It is just three months since I arrived. A part of the time we had beautiful weather, and I could walk on the road a little on sunshiny days, leaning upon my two sticks. But during the past five weeks my out-door exercise has been nil: the roads were too wet and rough. It has been almost constant fog, rain, wind; and the drip, drip, drip, of a mist that was wetter than rain. This, I think, has added a little rheumatism to give name to the pain and stiffness of joints and newly forming muscles. The change we are about to make will be a new departure for me—I shall have to try stairs. . . . But I shall have the dear companionship of Marjorie,[1] who has lived an ideal out-of-door life here. She will there begin to have regular lessons at home, or go to kindergarten. I have been reading to her Mary Proctor's "Starland," which by your thoughtful prompting she caused to be sent to me through her London publishers. I am so much obliged to you and to her for remembering the promise that I should have a copy. It is charming, and ought to have a wide sale. . . .

[1] Her grandchild.

I must stop; Vida has come for my mail, and is
going to the post-office on her bicycle. She and
Mr. Sidney are never so happy as when taking
long bicycle rides on these fine English country
roads.

With warmest greetings to Colonel Morse and
Ethel, and ever loving remembrance to you, dear
friend, I am, as always,

Ever yours,

J. C. C.

11 BARTON STREET, WEST KENSINGTON,
LONDON, January 29, 1899.

MY DEAR FRIEND:

I have been wondering these many days where
you are and how it is with you. How I have
wished that you were near by, and that we could
have taken some of my lonely, painful " duty "
walks upon crutches together. I miss your sympathy and ever ready kindness. . . . I suffer
terribly now with sore and swollen feet—the result
of pain, stiffness, strain in movement, and lack of
exercise. But I am stronger. I can now lift my
arms and brush my own hair. . . .

We are having beautiful weather just now. We
have had sunshine for a week, and people go
about announcing the fact with joy and surprise,
as if a new Saviour had arisen; all but the
Americans, newly come, who complain about
everything, rain or shine. . . .

J. C. C.

LONDON, Jan. 16, 1901.

DEAR FRIEND:

This letter is for the family. Poor as it will be, it will have to tell of all I would like to say to you, and for the thousand and one things I would like to tell of London and of the many kindnesses I have received. I had not expected to be here this winter, as you know, and ought not to be. The cold and the damp have developed rheumatism of a very severe type in my lame leg, and I suffer from pain and difficulty in walking. . . . I could, of course, obtain some mitigation of these conditions, but the same reason that compelled my return to London, Mr. P.'s actual failure, has so encroached upon my income—without a prospect of even partial recovery for a long time to come—as to make it almost equally difficult to live either in Switzerland, where, at Schinznach-les-Bains, I could receive so much benefit; or in London, or New York. I wish as I wished two years ago, that my accident had ended it, and saved all the pain and difficulty of solving a perpetual and insoluble problem. . . . It seems sometimes as if there were only two kinds of people in the world—those who ride over others roughshod, and those who are ridden over. The cruel accident that shattered me on that June day shattered my world. Life since then seems in the nature of a resurrection; every day a special gift, and every pleasant thing an act of Divine Providence.

22

Love to you all.   This is about myself.   Write soon and tell me all about yourselves.

Lovingly,
J. C. C.

From a Letter to Mrs. Christina J. Higley

LONDON, July —, 1899.

MY DEAR FRIEND:

. . . It seems as if everything had been taken from me but the friendship, the affection of women; and that manifests itself here as well as at home.   God bless them!   They have made all the brightness of my life.

Affectionately,
J. C. C.

From a Letter to Mrs. Catherine Young

LONDON, Sept. 3, 1895.

DEAREST MRS. YOUNG:

Your letter has been before my eyes many times. . . .

Keep up your courage and your faith in women and in the *old flag*.   I came across it the first time after I arrived, in a moment of extreme despondency.   It did me a world of good.   . . .   In

three weeks, if all goes well, I shall see you.   We
sail for New York on the 12th of this month.

Affectionately,

J. C. C.

From a Letter to Mrs. Harriet Nourse

. . . Oh, yes, I have made my will many
times; but some man always spoils it and I am
obliged to make it over.   I am not at all supersti-
tious about making a will.   My only trouble is
having nothing to leave.   I am fond of supersti-
tions—the little ones.   They give interest to life,
if you have to spend it in one place.   A little
unreason is less monotonous than the eternally
reasonable, and if it makes you happy for a
minute to see the moon over your right shoulder,
why not see it, and be unreasonably happy?

From a Letter to Mrs. Margaret W. Lemon

222 WEST 23RD STREET,
NEW YORK, Feb. 20, 1900.

MY DEAR MRS. LEMON:

I am very glad you are to formulate the resolution of thanks and appreciation of the work of the
Reception Committees.   Of course it goes without saying that it will be spread upon the minutes.

The work was altogether so fine and painstaking, and showed such thought, care, taste and judgment, that, apart from my personal pleasure in it, I felt exceedingly proud, and happy at the complete and beautiful result. . . . I am sorry you do not like "Current Events." To me "Current Topics" means the fag end of everything we know and have been obliged to read about in the papers. "Current Events" has a broader significance, and leaves out the trivial and vulgar.

Sincerely yours,
J. C. CROLY.

From a Letter to Mrs. E. S. Willard

BELLA-VISTA, BOSTON HARBOR, MASS.,
August 28, 1901.

. . . As yet I think I am still in London; or at least still in England. Crossing the Atlantic is not so much of an undertaking; less than taking a "trip" with "crossing" changes. Packing and unpacking, and the harassing "customs" are the worst features. There were only fifty-six passengers on the *Minneapolis*, but it took us from 8 A.M. to 1 P.M., in a pouring rain, to pass the argus-eyes of one hundred and eight inspectors, about two to each passenger.

In my case it seemed a bit ironical,—one of

Thomas Hardy's "Little Ironies," for a *rapid* American trustee had lost my whole capital during my absence. . . . The necessity for tying up the ragged ends and applying a test brought me home. But it is a trial, though I seem to have lost the power to be unhappy. Do you know what that means? Is that unarmed neutrality the serenity of Heaven?

I am as yet living in England. My thoughts are there, and my desire. I see you and a few others whom I love come and go, and I exchange the loving word, the kindly smile, the sympathetic look.

I am waiting for an indication of where I am to end my days. If my steps turn towards the isles of the sea, you will be a magnet to draw me, you with your spiritual beauty, and your constant, unfailing goodness. God bless you, and grant that I may see you again, and that we may gain the love, as well as the peace, that passeth all understanding.

Yours always,

J. C. CROLY.

Resolutions of Protest Offered by Mrs. Croly Through the Woman's Press Club

(From the Recording Secretary's Report)

At a special meeting of the Governing Board, held in the club rooms, 126 East 23rd street, Dec.

26, 1892, the following resolution proposed by the president was adopted.

Resolved: That the Woman's Press Club has learned with deep regret of the backward action of the Columbian University of Washington, in deciding to exclude women from its Medical Department, after ten years of co-education.

Resolved: That we unite with Pro-Re-Nata of Washington, D. C., in expressing an emphatic protest against this retrograde movement; that we earnestly hope that better counsels will prevail; that, at a time when so conservative an institution as the British Medical Association has voted to open its doors to women, the stigma of retrogression will not be allowed to rest upon the foremost school in the Capitol of the Nation.

Tributes of Friends

Jane Cunningham Croly

An Appreciation from Miriam Mason Greeley

In the joyful Christmas-tide of 1829, into the sweet influence of an English country home there came to life a blue-eyed, brown-haired maiden, whose sunny nature was destined to laugh with gladness of heart, or smile through falling tears, for more than seventy eventful years. "Jenny June" while yet a child came with her family to New York State, entering here an atmosphere well adapted to foster her activities and her power to work for the good of others. Her breadth of vision and her genial sympathy would have been evinced in any land or clime, but in the stimulating freedom of American thought her abilities developed to their best.

She found opportunity to plant the seeds of earnest thought, of which later she was to gather such a rich harvest in the confidence of her fellow-women. Her eager mind was a rich soil for the growth of ideas springing from her fertile brain; which led her to be both conservative and impetuous, grave or vivacious, ever fearless and versatile, all pervaded with the wholesome balance of quick penetration.

To her is due the tribute of praise for having borne the heat and burden of the day in the early development of women's clubs. Friends tried to persuade her to abandon her plans for organizing woman's varied abilities, ridicule assailed her most cherished hope, and the sarcasm of opponents barred the way. She lived to triumph in seeing her aims successful, and after thirty-five years of club life to be honored by one of the highest gifts in the power of the General Federation to offer—the honorary vice-presidency.

Mrs. Croly formulated in 1890 her well-matured plan for a general federation of women's clubs, and with the cordial assistance of the "Mother Club, Sorosis," issued the first call for representatives of women's clubs of all the States to meet.

Stimulated by the success of the General Federation, Mrs. Croly urged the formation of the New York State Federation, and assisted by Sorosis as the hostess, an invitation was issued to all the State clubs to be the guests of Sorosis at Sherry's, November, 1894.

Mrs. Croly's life-work as a writer had gone forward hand in hand with her club interests, and, having finished the foundation work of the two federations, she devoted her time to the preparation of her massive volume on the "Growth of the Woman's Club Movement," which is a monu-

MRS. CROLY
at the age of 18.

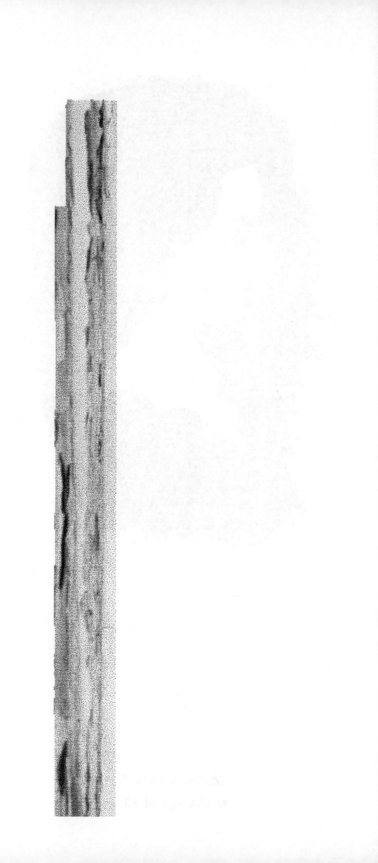

ment to her patient industry, and the only permanent record of the development of women's clubs in America.

She sleeps—but each woman who to-day shares the benefit and the responsive pleasure of club life, should place a leaf in the garland for "Jenny June."

From Marie Etienne Burns

"Work is a true savior, and the not knowing how is more the cause of idleness than the love of it."—MRS. CROLY.

THE idea of a State Industrial School for Girls originated with Mrs. Croly, and at a spring meeting of the Executive Committee of the New York State Federation of Women's Clubs, held in 1898, she suggested that the first work of the Philanthropic Committee for the year be an endeavor to establish a State Industrial School for wayward, not criminal, young girls of tenement-house neighborhoods. Soon after this Mrs. Croly met with a serious accident and was obliged to give up all active work. She decided to go to Europe, hoping to be benefited by a stay abroad. Just before her departure Mrs. Croly wrote asking me to present the proposed industrial-school plan to the Convention for its endorsement. The next day I called upon her to discuss matters. I found her confined to her sofa with a crutch beside her, and evidently suffering much pain; but she seemed to be thinking less about herself than about the work that was so close to her heart. She urged me to take up the work which she was regretfully obliged to abandon, and was most enthusiastic over it.

Mrs. Croly said: "Those who have worked among the poor in large cities are aware of the value of orderly and systematic industrial training for girls of irresponsible parentage, between the years of twelve and eighteen. These girls are often bright and attractive, but they are usually self-willed, lacking in judgment, and ignorant of every useful art, as well as of all social and domestic standards that lend themselves to the development of a true womanhood. Their homes are usually unworthy of the name, often scenes of disorder, not infrequently of violence, from which their only escape is the street. Their vanity and unbridled desire for low forms of pleasure expose them to all kinds of evil influences, and the first steps in a downward career are taken without at all knowing whither they lead. The most dangerous element in the lives of such girls is their ignorance. It bars all avenues to respectable employment and deprives them of self-respect, which grows with ability to maintain oneself and one's integrity in the face of adverse circumstances. In putting the knowledge of the simplest art or industry in possession of the untrained, unformed girl you supply an almost certain defence against that which lurks to destroy."

I fully agreed with Mrs. Croly. My many

years of experience as a worker among the poor
of New York City had taught me the importance, .
and indeed the necessity of just such a school, and
I gladly promised to carry forward the good work.

Mrs. Croly said in parting: '' I can truly say
that during the whole of my working life in New
York, a period of more than forty years, my heart
has bled for these poor neglected, untrained girls,
who yet have the elements of a divine womanhood
and motherhood within them, though undeveloped
and hidden by the rankest weeds and growth.''

At the Convention in New York City, held in
1901, I presented the Industrial School project,
and the plan received the unanimous endorsement
of all those present. It was, however, deemed
wiser to omit the word ''wayward,'' as the school
was to be preventive and in no sense reformatory.
A Committee was formed, of which Mrs. Croly
was made Honorary Chairman; and the work
upon a State Industrial School for Girls was
begun.

It was my desire as Acting Chairman of the
Committee that the movement should carry at all
times the banner bearing the name of its inceptor,
a name that would always suggest not failure but
success. While seemingly insurmountable obstacles at once arose, they were more or less
overcome as the preparations and work of the
Committee progressed. And at the time of Mrs.
Croly's death the project had reached a point more

hopeful than assured, resulting in the establishment of at least one school which should stimulate the State Legislature into a realization of the needs of the young girls of the tenement-house neighborhoods, so that some time in the future there might be provided through State legislation, on a broad plan, the State Industrial or Trade School for Girls, the idea of which was conceived by Jenny June.

From Mrs. Croly's Letter to Mrs. Burns, Relative to the Proposed Industrial School for Girls

222 WEST 23RD STREET,
Feb. 28, 1900.

MY DEAR MRS. BURNS:

There is only one point that I would have emphasized, and that I do not find included in your otherwise excellent statement. It is the moral influence of a training for self-support. Ignorance and idleness lead to vice and crime; and a Technical Training School would do more to remedy the Social Evil and raise the standard of morals than all other influences combined. The fact that work is the great purifier is what I wish could have been embodied in the plan presented.

Yours with real regard.

J. C. C.

From Izora Chandler

How can one picture all that this one woman was to the hundreds of other women who loved her: the gentle demeanor, the thoughtful conversation, the high thinking evidenced not less in her choice of subject than in the fitness of word and phrase which gave a distinctive charm to all her utterances, whether public or private?

When first meeting Mrs. Croly one could hardly believe that so gentle-voiced, slight a creature could have accomplished the pioneering accredited to her in the enlargement of the mental life of women. Drawn to her at the first greeting one was soon convinced of the hidden forcefulness of her nature which could be likened to the resistless, unyielding under-current, rather than to the wave which visibly and noisily assails the shore.

Present or absent, the thought of her was magnetic. While charming the heart she convinced the mind with argument. Her power did not absorb and minify; it enlarged, enlivened, and became a source of inspiration. After talking with her, impossibilities became possible to the timid, the diffident were encouraged to dare, and those who were strong at coming went away valorous. Her dignity and ready decision when presiding over a public assembly were noteworthy. She became a stateswoman in whatever concerned her sex; an earnest soul pleading for love among co-workers, and for more and yet more of love, for only in that atmosphere can the heart of woman come into its rightful sovereignty, urging that slights be forgotten, aggressions overlooked, and that the fair mantle of love be spread tenderly over all.

An earnest devotee of the best and highest in art, she seemed to have an insatiable desire after the beautiful; and was never more serene and lucid of mind than when considering this scheme, and encouraging with rich appreciation those who were in the field.

Her store of knowledge was phenomenal. She was a constant learner, an unwearied seeker after wisdom. When those who had given special study to any subject addressed the house over which she presided, they received her most flattering attention, and in the brief afterword of the chairman she indicated intimate knowledge of the matter in hand, often giving comprehensive data and suggesting fresh lines for consideration. No wonder that the finest minds were attracted to her; that thinkers desired her acceptance of their thoughts; that active workers sought her coöperation and leadership. Quiet and forceful; competent as a critic, but ready with encouragement; simple in manner, easily approached; patient with

13

those who appealed to her, seeking rather than waiting to be sought; abundantly appreciative of others, her memory becomes an abiding impulse towards high and generous thought, towards simple, worthy living.

From Janie C. P. Jones

BEFORE my friend's last trip to England I went to bid her good-bye, and among her parting words were the following which I never can forget:

"I dislike going so far from my friends. To me they are the most precious things on earth, the greatest gift the world can bestow; to me they have been like flowers all along my path, and their sweet odor of influence has made me better every day. I cannot prize them too highly, for all I am I owe to them."

To have known one who so highly appreciated the value of friendship, who knew the true meaning of the word "friend," and who possessed the rare gift of knowing how to retain friends, was an inspiration, and an influence which added to the value of life. I think of her now as having "gone into her garden to gather lilies for her Beloved."

From Catherine Weed Barnes Ward

My task is at once sad and pleasant: sad, because I speak of a dearly loved and lost friend; pleasant, because I am asked to bear my testimony as to her worth.

Mrs. Croly's friendship and unselfish kindness began with my entrance over twenty years ago into club life, and from then onward she was continually urging and helping me towards increased intellectual effort. Through her active inspiration I joined Sorosis, the Woman's Press Club of New York, and other American organizations, as well as the Society of American Women in London, the Women Journalists of London, and various English organizations, besides taking part in the International Congress of Women held in London three or four years ago.

Mrs. Croly lived constantly in two generations, her own and the next one; her wonderful mental vitality setting the paces of many pulses besides those which stirred her own brain. I know much of the actual labor she accomplished for her sex, both here and in England, but even nobler than that was the high ideal she set them in her own life and the inspiration of her personality to younger women.

To those she called special friends her loyalty was unswerving, true as the needle to the pole, and as one blest with such friendship I feel the influence of her beautiful, unselfish living will be ever with me, though something has gone out of my life, never to be replaced. Her daughter, Mrs. Vida Croly Sidney, worthily carries on the traditions and work of her noble mother, and her friends feel that in her there is a living tie between the untiring spirit laboring now, we may well believe, in another existence and the work so loved by that spirit while on earth.

A true heart, a generous nature, a broad mind, and keen mental acumen are qualities that do not die with their possessor; they bless the world to which she has gone and that she left behind.

We can best honor her memory by carrying on her work and by leaving the world better and happier for our having lived in it.

From a Letter to the Memorial Committee from Sara J. Lippincott (Grace Greenwood)

I FEEL Mrs. Croly's death very deeply. The sacred holiday season, dedicated from time immemorial to household joy and mirth, and calling for Christian gratitude and hope, was already saddened by bereavements, and her death—absolutely unlooked for by me—made it melancholy and mournful.

"She should have died hereafter." I did not dream when I saw her last that she was to solve the great mystery before me. Though feeble, there seemed so much of the old energetic, enthusiastic self about her; and I parted from her hoping to see her soon in renewed health and strength.

She always had a peculiar fascination for me: her soft, sweet voice; her strong though quiet will; her unfailing faith in all things good; her loyalty to her sex. I think her pass-word to the realm of rest and reward must have been, "I loved my fellow-woman."

35 LOCKWOOD AVENUE, NEW ROCHELLE,
January 6, 1902.

From a Letter to the Memorial Committee from Jennie de la M. Lozier

MRS. CROLY was a woman of uncommon intuition and sympathy. She took wide and far-reaching views of woman's possible development and usefulness. She believed in organization as a factor in this development, and spared no effort to form and maintain, even at personal sacrifice, the woman's club or federation. She was always generous and warm-hearted, of boundless hospitality, never more genially herself than when her friends gathered about her in her attractive home and she could make them happy. I shall always recall with pleasure the rare moments when she talked with me of her real life, her hopes and her plans. I believe that she constantly exerted a noble influence, and that she stood for all that makes for woman's unselfish helpfulness, courage and independence.

NEW YORK, February 10, 1902.

From Genie H. Rosenfeld

IN the early days of the Woman's Press Club, when it was divided upon the question of a suitable meeting place, and undisciplined members were resigning in appreciable numbers, Mrs. Croly surprised me one day by declaring that the club had never been stronger than it was at that hour.

"Why, Mrs. Croly!" I exclaimed, "we have only a handful of women left."

"My dear," she said, "we have lopped off all our dead wood. The branches that remain may be few, but they are vigorous, and from them will spring up a tree that will be a glory to us."

This little saying of Mrs. Croly's has come back to me and been of use many times, and it has often enabled me to understand the benefit of lopping off dead wood and starting anew.

Contributed to the New York *Tribune* by S. A. Lattimore

THE sad announcement of the death of Mrs. Jane Cunningham Croly recalls a delightful incident of several summers ago when I had the pleasure of meeting her at Long Branch.

In the course of a most interesting conversation I ventured to ask her to give me the origin of her well-known *nom-de-plume* of " Jenny June." In her bright, sympathetic way, which all who knew her can describe, she said:

" Yes, I will tell you. In my early girlhood I knew a young clergyman who was in the habit of occasionally visiting our house. One day he came to bid us good-bye, saying that he was going to a Western city to reside. As he bid me good-bye he gave me a little book. It was a volume of B. F. Taylor's poems, called 'January and June.' The little book opened of itself at a page containing verses entitled ' The Beautiful River.' An introductory paragraph read thus: ' On such a night, in such a June, who has not sat side by side with somebody for all the world like Jenny June? Maybe it was years ago, but it was some time. Maybe you had quite forgotten it, but you will be the better for remembering. Maybe she

has gone on before where it is June all the year,
and never January at all,—that God forbid.   There
it was, and then it was, and thus it was.'   This
stanza was marked in pencil:

'Jenny June,' then I said, 'let us linger no more
    On the banks of the beautiful river ;
 Let the boat be unmoored, and muffled the oar,
    And we'll steal into heaven together.
 If the angel on duty our coming descries
 You have nothing to do but throw off the disguise
    That you wore when you wandered with me;
 And the sentry will say: "Welcome back to the skies,
    We long have been waiting for thee!"''

On the margin was written, ' You are the Juniest
Jenny I know.'

"The years of my girlhood passed on, and with
their passing faded away all memory of the young
minister.   Later there came to me, as I suppose
there comes to every young girl, the impulse to
write, and when some early efforts of mine were
judged worthy to be published, I was confronted
for the first time with the question of a signature.
Shrinking from seeing my own name in print, by
some witchery of memory the words 'Jenny June'
suddenly occurred to me, and that, as you know,
has been my name ever since."

After a little pause Mrs. Croly said: " Now
that I have answered your question I must tell
you something else.   Thirty years after I had as-

sumed my *nom-de-plume* a gray-haired stranger called at my house one day and asked to see me. The name he gave recalled no one I had ever known, and in meeting there was no recognition on either side. But he proceeded in a straightforward way to explain the object of his visit: 'For the last thirty years,' he said, 'since my removal from this city, I have lived in the West; naturally, I have been a constant reader of Eastern papers, and particularly have I read every article I have ever seen bearing the signature of "Jenny June." I have made many efforts, but always without success, to ascertain who she was, and whether the name was real or fictitious. Somehow I have never forgotten the little girl I knew before I went West, and to whom I gave a little volume of poems with something written on a page that contained a stanza that I greatly admired about "Jenny June." I have wondered if she had become the famous writer, and upon my return to my native city, after so long an absence, I have sought you simply to ask if you are that little girl.' "

The Fairies' Gifts

By Ellen M. Staples

To an English home one bright Yuletide
While Christmas bells rang loud and wide

Came a babe with the gentle eyes of a dove
And a face as fair as a thought of love.

" Now, God be thanked," the old nurse cried,
" That the child is born at Christmas-tide;

" For the blessed sake of Mary's Son
God's benison falls on lives begun

" When Christmas music fills the air
And men are joyful everywhere.

" And as to Him came Wise Men three
Offering gifts on bended knee

" So to one born at the Holy Time
On land or sea, in every clime,

" Come three Good Fairies, and each one bears
A gift to brighten the coming years."

The pallid mother gently smiled
And looked upon her tender child.

" Good nurse, the legend is full sweet;
And I lay my babe at His dear feet

" Whose human Sonhood is aware
Of the painful bliss that mothers bear.

" I can well believe that heaven may
Send gifts to the child of Christmas Day."

Tired by her flight from Paradise
The baby shut her wondering eyes,

Nor knew that 'round the cradle stood,
To bless the babe, three Fairies good.

The First bent over the cradle head;
" These are my gifts to her," she said:

" A sunny nature, a voice of song,
And may faithful friends uncounted throng!"

The Second murmured in accents low:
" The path will be steep and rough, I know,

" So I give her a heart that is brave and strong,
That will patiently work, though the way be long;

" And though life may fill them with toil and care
Her hands shall weaker ones' burdens share."

Then stood the Third for a moment's space
To thoughtfully gaze on the baby face,

And over her own a radiance came
As she softly said: " My gift is a name.

" Though born while the earth lies spread with
　　snow
The babe is a summer-child, and so

" The sunny nature, the voice of song,
The helpful hands, true heart and strong

" With Nature's self should be in tune,
Sweet child, I name thee Jenny June."

From Margaret Ravenhill

JANE CUNNINGHAM CROLY left upon the last century an ineffaceable record. For industrious and successful work in journalism she probably had no peer. In a speech before the Woman's Press Club not long since, she said: "When a woman has written enough to fill a room, she feels like burning it instead of preserving it in scrap-books." Probably no woman of her day and generation has done more or better work than our "Jenny June." No woman had more diversity of gifts; she was equally at home in the editorial chair, or the reportorial office; as a speaker she excelled. In the old days we who knew her best would sometimes notice a hesitancy of speech that would occasionally cloud a brilliant idea; but if she hesitated she was never lost, and the idea was worth waiting for. She was always clear, logical, forceful in expression, and exhaustive in argument. Thoroughness seems the word to express the character of Mrs. Croly. She was quick to catch the meaning of the uttered thoughts of others, keen in analysis, and executive in all work. Witness the many organizations which she helped originate. Her long years of rule as president of Sorosis were of inestimable value to that "mother of women's clubs." Her great "History of the Club Movement" should be in the hands of every woman in the land.

Of Mrs. Croly's personality it is a pleasure to speak. Every woman who enjoyed the privilege of her friendship felt the magnetism and charm of a rare nature; while, with all her force and power, there was a childishness about her that impressed one with the idea that the naiveté and innocence of childhood had never been wholly lost in the woman. I think it was in some measure owing to the fact that she was so near-sighted that there was a kind of appealing hesitancy about her movements that impelled you to her aid.

Mrs. Croly's home was one of refinement and good taste in every detail, and there she was at her best. Always a charming hostess, she made every guest feel that he or she was the one most eagerly expected; there were the hearty greeting, the few low words of welcome, the sunny smile that transformed her face into positive beauty. Her Sunday evenings at home came nearer in character to the French salon than any others in New York. There were the most delightful people to be met: the gifted minds of our own land and Europe were among her guests. But Mrs. Croly's proudest boast was that she was a woman's woman.

From T. C. Evans, in the New York *Times*

WHEN I joined the *World* staff of writers, in 1860, a few weeks after the foundation of that journal, I found Jenny June already there. She did not often appear in the office in person, the lady auxiliary in journalism not being so familiar a figure as it now is, and she had not yet adopted her pretty *nom-de-plume*, but her husband, David G. Croly, held an official post on the staff as city editor, and her contributions, which were invariably well written and interesting, appeared from the first in the *World* columns, and as the years went on while she and Mr. Croly remained associated with it, with increasing frequency. They were written by a woman mainly for women, and the maids and matrons of her country over all its area from ocean to ocean and from "lands of sun to lands of snow" have never been addressed by one of their sex whom they came to know better or to hold in higher esteem. Her work assumed no pretentious or high importance, but was sweet and wholesome, sensible, and a mirror of the nature out of which it proceeded. The name Jenny June, which she adopted a few years later, became a beloved household word throughout the

land, perhaps more widely known than that of
any lady journalist who has ever wrought in it.

Mrs. Croly's social dispositions and her aptitude for gathering interesting people around her
were gracious endowments of nature's bestowal,
as strongly marked in her youth as in her maturer
years, when she gradually came to have a wider
stage on which to display them. Her pretty little
drawing-rooms, somewhere on the west side near
Grove Street, are well remembered by me, and
first and last I met in them a goodly number of
people well worthy to be remembered, some with
their trophies of success yet to win, but their merit
divined by their clever hostess, perhaps before it
had obtained any full recognition elsewhere.
Many also came who had won their spurs and
epaulets and shone bravely in the bright glitter
of both. In her little unpretending salon of that
day might be met the brilliant young Edmund
Clarence Stedman, in the morning glow of his
poetic fame; Bayard Taylor, risen into the mid-
forenoon of his fame, with his Orient lyrics published and his translation of " Faust " well begun;
perhaps Phœbe and Alice Cary, though on this
point I cannot be certain, and many another of
note and distinction in that time, her hospitality
taking in all arts, and all the presentable workers
in them, so that poets, painters, sculptors, singers,
actors were equally welcome, as were those who
brought to her only their bright young counte-

nances and winning smiles. Her later drawing-rooms, when she had removed up town, nearer to the Mayfair of society, became widely celebrated, and she founded something perhaps as near to a salon modeled after the traditional Parisian standards as any that America has known.

Mrs. Croly is recognized as the chief among the founders of Sorosis, the most celebrated woman's club in the world, and parent of the innumerable organizations of like sect which have sprung up since their renowned progenitor became with fewer vicissitudes and trials than might have been anticipated firmly planted on its feet and attested its self-supporting and self-reliant character. No social development of the modern period is more striking than the swift multiplication of women's clubs, not in this country alone, but in others, and they have shown a power of beneficent work most advantageous to the community at large, which even the most sanguine among their promoters could not have anticipated. They have also shown that women can legislate and administrate and rise to the point of order and lay things on the table in a manner as parliamentary and self-restrained as men. For such testimony the world should be thankful, as it never got anything of the kind before. Among the founders of this now most impressive group of social organizations no name stands out more brightly and conspicuously than that of Jane Cunningham Croly.

Her recent death, though a surprise and shock to her innumerable friends, came when she had passed her seventy-second birthday, and it cannot therefore be said that she passed away with her work uncompleted. It was fully and most worthily performed, and was the fruit of a systematic diligence never remitted, and in which few of her sex in any period could have exceeded her. Her memory is fragrant as the month from which she took her *nom-de-plume*, and will at least be cherished by those whom her gentle discourse, continued for more than a generation, has entertained and instructed.

From St. Clair McKelway, in the Brooklyn *Eagle*

THE death of Jane Cunningham Croly, noticed in Tuesday's *Eagle*, involves the loss of a
woman of leadership who put a good deal of help
into others' lives. Born in 1829, she began at
seventeen to write for newspapers. Her topics
were, for a wonder, practical, the young too generally beginning with abstract, academical or rec-
ondite subjects.   Hers were '' fashions '' in dress,
fads in food, fancies and foibles in decoration etc.
From them she advanced to more philosophical or
general fields, but on all she wrote was the stamp
of applicability to contemporaneous life.

In the middle, later, and more genial period of
her life she did more talking than writing.   And
her talking was always earnest, direct, sincere,
with a gleam of hope and a note of wisdom in it
—the union of experience and reflection.   Had it
been reported it would have made for her a literary
name: but she was content, or constrained, to
limit her work to the platform, or to the circle of
existence affected by it.

As a clubwoman Mrs. Croly achieved the emi-
nence almost of a pioneer.   It can be shown that
a club or two of women had a titular beginning

before "Sorosis," but that was the original society started by her on the theory that there were opportunities and conditions in club life, on an educational or literary basis, of which women could well avail themselves. Mrs. Croly sympathized with the more earnest purposes entering into her idea, and was in little related to any sensational, spectacular, or faddish features that may here or there become attached to it. She was a believer in seriousness, an exemplar of industry, a devotee to system, and a very remarkably punctual, effective and straightforward writer. Her flight was never very high, but it was always progressive, and her regulation of her pen by the precise rules that govern presswork was entitled to distinct praise. She could always be trusted to keep within her topic and herself behind it, and she understood the art of putting things to her public in a way to discover to them their own thoughts as well as to denote her own.

To David G. Croly, her husband, long a newspaper man of admitted power and executive force, Mrs. Croly was a constant help, as he too was to her. From him she learned not a little of her topical discernment and technical knack. He was never afraid of ability in whomever found, and he rejoiced that the sex of his wife, and the novel fact that she was the first woman in America to write daily for publication, gave to her and her subjects a vogue he and his could not command in a world of more and mainly personal work. She survived him twelve years. Their union was not made any less congenial by marked dissimilarity of convictions on cardinal subjects.

Mrs. Croly was the recipient of many evidences of the honor and affection in which her own sex held her, and beyond doubt the organizations of which she was the inspiring force will pay to her memory the tributes her disinterestedness and abilities deserved, exercised as she always was for so long with projects nearly related to the better equipment of effective womanhood for the conditions and conduct of life. Her death at seventy-two, after not a little suffering and not a few sorrows, was not unexpected, though it will be sincerely and widely regretted. In her last years she was happily made aware of the love and tenderness towards her which she had richly earned by service, counsel, and example to the lives of others.

From Laura Sedgwick Collins

DEAR Friend, dear Helper, passed from earth
To heaven, in earthly grace, I here
Would give to thee homage sincere
And memory sweet. Thy ever kindly word
Has oft the sad heart warmed,
The drooped head raised, and thy sustaining hand
A fainting purpose thrilled
To better courage, firmer aim.

In that far realm where spirits meet
And greet with message mystic, there
Thou must, in sweet commune
Receive reward for earthly deeds.
Thy heart ne'er knew the unkind throb,
Was ever gentle, firm and true;
Whate'er the cause, if once espoused
Thou to thy watchword held thyself.

Throughout our land, in city, town,
Thy name beloved remains alive;
Alive in hearts, alive in minds,—
For thou hadst heart and brain as well
To touch the soul and win the thought.
Thy work for woman stands unspoiled;
Untouched by vanity or marred by pride,
Unsullied by a thought of self,

A generous impulse toward thy sex—
A woman's word for woman's need.
And so thy name in fragrance fine
Bespeaks again returning June,—
The spring of promise, budding hope!
The cypress changes to the rose,—
The rose of dawn, the rose of heaven;
And both are thine and thine the crown
All jewelled o'er with thy good deeds—
Deeds of mercy, deeds of love,
Are with us still though thou art gone!

From Mary Coffin Johnson

MANY years before I personally knew Mrs. Croly she was at the height of her useful public life; the imprint of her hand and mind in contemporary literature was an evident fact, and she had become a conspicuous figure in the ranks of well-known women. It is therefore my privilege to speak of her last few years, when the golden light of achievement gilded the eventide of her eventful life.

Having had the peculiar advantage of sitting beside her for six years as an officer of the Woman's Press Club I am thoroughly aware of her sincerity, and of the singleness of heart which actuated her motives in behalf of women. She believed that every united effort that raises the personal standard of thought and purpose is of the utmost importance. It was her earnest desire that women should live lofty and useful lives. She frequently laid stress upon this manner of life, and at such times her temperament seemed charged with sympathetic interest in young women journalists. "Unity in Diversity," the motto adopted by the General Federation of Women's Clubs, is a fitting expression of the broad conceptions she brought into club life; in-

deed, her success in bringing women of unequal
social position and essentially different callings,
into harmonious relationship and unity of purpose
was markedly characteristic.

During her last years women's clubs became
more than ever of absorbing interest to her, claim-
ing the complete devotion of her broad mind.
The untiring devotion she had already given to
this part of her life's activities had established her
fame, and this fame will ever be exceptionable,
for her work can never be duplicated.

The growing spirit of helpfulness and friendli-
ness which inspires women's organizations, the
manifold opportunities of various kinds which
they afford, and the excellent results which follow could, she thought, scarcely be estimated.
" Club life for women," she would say, " requires
no justification. When we enter our club rooms
we leave behind us much of the rubbish of the
world. The richest, fullest development of life
flows through the better social relations, and from
times of old has been uplifting." " It is not
merely that we need one another," she would de-
clare, " but that the sense of kinship is healthful;
it inspires the larger love, and creates a stronger
relationship. It seems to be God's method of
helping humankind to the higher and more
perfect life."

On various occasions, when only members of
the club were present, she would lay aside the

formality of the presiding member, and, assuming
the familiar manner of addressing us, pour forth
her lofty ideals for women, unconsciously testify-
ing that the secret spring of her actions was her
love for her own sex. Though the words were
always spoken with gentle calmness, and in a
tone of womanly softness, something in her pas-
sionate sincerity would, like the effect of a magnet, attract every listener, and a spell of silence
would fall upon us. In all that she said we dis-
cerned the Divine Principle.

There were those who, from their own view-
points, carped at what they heard and saw, but a
person even of Mrs. Croly's temperament and
courage, placed amid the recurring action and
reaction of a life of much publicity, cannot, of
course, please every one. It would be surprising
if in her long career she had not manifested human imperfections, and had not sometimes made
mistakes; she would have been more than human
had she not.

It was no easy task for her to stem the tide of
difficulties and oppositions from without, for from
first to last of her diligent life she had many trials
to endure. Both sunbeam and shadow crossed
her pathway; but her errors were not uncommon
to humankind; moreover, she was very patient
under misconception. " It is always fair," said
Henry Ward Beecher, " to credit a man at his
best,—let his enemies tell of his worst." Another

writer remarks: " To get a true idea of any character we must seize upon its higher forming element, that to which it naturally tends."

Hers was far from an impulsive nature, yet there were times when Mrs. Croly suddenly revealed in a marked way her true, deep instincts. While on a visit to this country on one occasion, Madame Antoinette Sterling, a concert singer in England, was a guest of the Woman's Press Club. She was asked to sing for us, and responded with " The Lost Chord." In answer to an encore she sang a ballad of her own composition, called "The Sheepfold." Mrs. Croly was visibly affected by the words; seldom had she ever manifested more feeling. When the song was ended she quickly rose, and in a tremulous voice exclaimed: " Does not this say to us that if even *one* were outside, the whole strength of the universe would be brought to bear upon it, to bring it into the fold! "

In 1897 Mrs. Croly was honored by the General Federation of Women's Clubs by the appointment to write the "History of the Woman's Club Movement in America," an undertaking that required exceptionable ability. The vast amount of mental energy and wearing labor she put into this work, added to the past years of constant application to literary and other interests, told seriously upon her health. Her nervous system had become exceedingly susceptible, and it was evident that her good constitution was beginning to break down.

However, the indomitable energy she possessed, and her trained capacity for work enabled her to continue until the large volume was finished and given to the public.

Early in June, 1898, Mrs. Croly had a serious fall in which she fractured her hip, and she was confined to her room for many weeks. Though she possessed unusual power of endurance, her lessening strength could no longer bear the strain upon the delicate frame, and her rallying power was perceptibly diminished. As the fracture slowly healed she but feebly met the physical exertion necessary to go about on crutches. Even then it was impossible for her to take life serenely; she was restlessly eager to be up and doing. When she could be removed with safety, which was not until the third of September, she went abroad with her daughter, Mrs. Vida Croly Sidney, who had come over from England for her, and she spent a year in London and the vicinity. In August, 1899, they were in Switzerland, and Mrs. Croly took the baths at Schinznach-les-Bains. She returned to America the following September, and remained in New York through the winter of 1899–1900. The change agreed with her, but her health cannot be said to have improved, and she was still very infirm. Her natural affection and interest in the Woman's Press Club led her to attend its meetings, whenever she was able, going there in the carriage sent for her. On the 12th of

May she was present at a club meeting, and gave
us an informal talk, which proved to be her parting address, though at the time we knew it not.
That day her words were full of significance. She
expressed herself with fervor, chiefly on the importance of clubwomen bearing a large measure
of love and good-will towards one another, and of
the cultivation of the tie of divine charity. With
earnestness she urged again that we should stand
" hand to hand to exercise patience in judgment,
and to be slow in criticism." "It is God-like,"
she said, " to forgive. Remember," she continued, " that all that is good in this life emanates
from love; that it is the very best thing that this
life affords, and that there is nothing on earth that
can take the place of its ministry. Love has no
limitations, and if you give the best talent you
possess to your club it will give it back to you.
Club life is often misunderstood, it is true,—but,"
she slowly added, " there is nothing in this world
entirely perfect." She spoke touchingly of the
personal sense of loneliness she felt; that although
she was a woman among many women she lived
many a lonely hour; and she wished it well understood that the love and friendship of clubwomen was to her the most precious thing in her
life. In closing she emphasized the counsel she
had given, to be " United and conciliatory in our
relations with each other; to be just; to suspend
judgment; and to wait long and trust God who

knows all.   He," she declared, " will not misun-
derstand you."

At the end of May she returned to England.
Though nature had not become victorious over
her feebleness, and she was still almost helpless
from the effect of the accident of 1898, she heroic-
ally overcame these physical conditions as far as
she was able.   Something continually impelled
her onward.   She attended the International
Congress of Women held during the Paris Ex-
position of that year, and then went on to Ober-
Ammergau to the Passion Play, accompanied by
Mrs. Sidney; and then returned to England,
where she stayed until the 27th of July, 1901,
when she again sailed for New York, business
matters requiring her presence in this country.

On her arrival in August from the second visit
abroad, the grave facts that her health was not
established, and that her time here was not to
be long, were soon evident to her friends.   The
struggle of nature not only had begun, the
shadow was even now sweeping near.   She appeared at the November business meeting of the
Woman's Press Club, accompanied by an at-
tendant, and took the chair, but she was so much
exhausted by the effort that her nurse easily per-
suaded her to come away.   During the following
four weeks her prostration and decline were steady.

As the final day of her human infirmity approached, she expressed to the close friend who

sat beside her a timid shrinking, common to all human nature, from the passage out of this life. It may be counted a special mercy that, as it afterwards proved, she need not have had any disquietude concerning the inevitable moment, for a few hours before the closing scene she fell into a state of coma, and passed beyond so quietly and tranquilly that she did not herself know when the moment came. She entered the world of infinite repose in the forenoon of December 23, 1901.

The funeral service was held in the Church of the Transfiguration, Mrs. Croly's friends gathering from far and near to pay their last tributes of love and regard. The women's clubs and societies of Manhattan, Brooklyn, and the suburbs, were represented in large numbers, and every seat in the church was filled.

Mrs. Croly lies at rest beside her husband, David G. Croly, in the beautiful cemetery near Lakewood, New Jersey.

"Yon 's her step . . . an' she 's carryin' a licht in her hand; a see it through the door."

15

From Caroline M. Morse

As Chairman of the Memorial Committee it is my privilege to add my memories of Mrs. Croly to those which have preceded. Mine are not of her club interests, nor of her identification with the woman's club movement. So much has been written, and so well, regarding these public phases of her life that it would seem almost officious for me to add a stone to the already piled up cairn; I write rather of my friend as my family knew her in her home, surrounded by husband and children.

It was in 1880 that we first knew Mr. and Mrs. Croly, and the acquaintance soon became an intimacy that lasted for twenty-three years. They were living in their own house in Seventy-first street, an artistically furnished house, an ideal home full of a sweet domesticity.

Intimate as we were it was frequently our privilege to gather with the family at their Sunday evening supper, when Mrs. Croly was as completely the "house-mother" fulfilling the homely duties of the table, as, an hour later, she was the gracious, though more formal hostess receiving in her drawing-room the usual Sunday night throng of old friends and the strangers of distinction who, chancing to be in town, were fortunate enough to have letters of introduction to her. I see her slight figure moving from group to group, and the low English voice and sweet smile with which she encouraged her visitors to speak of themselves, and, if they were foreigners, of their missions to this country. A characteristic act of hers was to carry around a little silver tray on which there might be several glasses of a dainty punch, the base of which was a light, non-alcoholic wine. This she offered to friends whom she desired particularly to honor, and the act had all the significance of the Russian custom of breaking bread and eating salt with the host. These Sunday evenings at home, which were a feature of the society in which she moved, were continued until a short time before her death, or until she was incapacitated by illness.

My friend had none of the usual failings of the traditionary ''emancipated woman''; she would sit down to her basket on an afternoon and take up a bit of household sewing with the same spirit and aptitude that had guided her in the forenoon in the writing of an editorial article or the preparation of a paper to be read before a club.

I recall with especial joy the long walks we used to take together. After a day of wearisome work, it was one of her great delights to leave the piled-up desk and find herself in the street, her arm linked in mine. At such times much of her talk was ravishing speculation upon things seen and unseen. It was as if, released for the moment from the pressure of work, her mind sprang into a world removed from the practical and immediate, to revel in contemplation of the divine. Yet she was no visionary, and the world of sight held her cheerful allegiance. Hers was never "the dyer's hand subdued to what it works in," and this is the more remarkable since she never relinquished work, even for our beloved walks, without a mild protest at laying aside her pen. One afternoon I called, intending to take her out for one of our "play-hours," but I failed to find her in her apartment. Next morning the post brought me this note:

"MY DEAR FRIEND:

"I was so glad to get your card, and so sorry to miss you. It was just that hour out-of-doors with you that I was longing for. I have been so long away, and since my return have been so busy with much detail of correspondence that in quantity is always more or less depressing, that I needed a sight of you to tone me up and restore my standard. I have also taken advantage of enforced quiet to brace up for an heroic two weeks of dentistry, and have therefore been in absolute retirement and upon baby diet of the most innocuous description. . . .

"I am afraid this recapitulation will take away all desire to repeat your effort in my direction.

But I trust that this may find you in a missionary humor, and that you will see that I need 'looking after'—a far stronger motive with most women than friendship, is n't it? Anyway, come again soon, won't you? Afternoon is our gadding time, you know.

"Really and lovingly your friend.

"P. S.—This note will show that I truly have not command of all my faculties and need a human tonic."

All out-of-doors was dear to her. Trees were to her as men — rooted, and she often naïvely talked to them as if to friends while we strolled in the twilight. Her love of nature even seemed to affect her choice of diet, for she preferred simply prepared dishes and the natural foods. This was doubtless due in part to her unmixed Old World nationality and to her early surroundings in rural England: as she was in girlhood, so, in spite of the complex life of this distracting New World, she remained to the last.

My friend dwelt lovingly upon anniversaries; the true spirit of Christmas entered her heart at every Yuletide season, and her gifts showed generous care in selection and in the dainty wrappings in which they were sent to us. She delighted in the Christmas and Thanksgiving dinners, but St. Valentine's was the dearest, as it was the anniversary of her marriage. This the Woman's Press Club of New York has always observed as the date of its annual dinner.

She had a keen sense of humor, yet never did she forget herself either in posing or pranks, for hers was the unerring sense of the fitness of things. An instance of her ready wit comes to me: Soon after her return from her last visit to England she came to us to stay for a few days. It was in September, three months before her death. On Sunday evening several friends dropped in, and from general conversation we drifted into singing some of the old songs. Now and then she would add her own low tones to our untrained vocalizing, crooning or cantillating the tune as if she were musing aloud. We had been singing for a full hour, she, with crutch near at hand, sitting apart from us at the open window. We had just sung one of her favorites, the old ballad "Far Away," and were beginning another with all the energy of amateurs when it occurred to me that Mrs. Croly might be tired and ready to go to her room for the night. Bending over I whispered, "Come, dear, you must be weary of all this." She turned slowly in her chair, and looking up into my face, smiling whimsically, said: "Oh, no, not yet! I am enjoying the music just as if it were good!"

I have already intimated that the home life of the family was happy. There existed between husband and wife a genuine congeniality in tastes and pursuits; yet between any two minds when both are strong and original there will generally be a divergence; and it has always seemed to me that the origin of Sorosis might be traced by the psychological analyst to some such divergence between Mrs. Croly's lines of intellectual development and those of her equally gifted husband, David G. Croly. The power of initiative was strong in each of these two, and in each it produced excellent though differing results.

It is cause for regret that Mrs. Croly did not write more in her latter years, when her native wisdom had ripened in the soil of a rich experience.

Her philosophy was the fruit of a rightly-lived, useful life, and even after the distressing accident which lamed her, her enthusiasm never waned, but rather seemed intensified and glorified. Seldom do the heart and brain work together as did hers. She will ever stand to those who knew her as a fine specimen of a rare type. She had convictions, and she had the courage to uphold them. She hated shams and hypocrisy with the vigor of Carlyle. The bravery of her public life was matched by the beauty of her private life. Good and Truth were her watchwords. "Good has faculty," says Swedenborg, "but not determinate except by truth. Determinate faculty is actual power." In the dear friend whom we here commemorate, faculty was determinate.

Brave and honest pleader for woman; true, tender, sincere friend, you fought the good fight well; the world is better for your work, and among your saddest survivors are those whom you smote with a deserved pen-stroke, or with spoken words, who have long since given you grateful thanks.

C. M. M.

L' Envoi

She cut a path through tangled underwood
   Of old traditions out to broader ways.
She lived to hear her work called brave and good,
   But oh! the thorns, before the crown of bays.
The world gives lashes to its pioneers
Until the goal is reached—then deafening cheers.

                 ELLA WHEELER WILCOX.